Mike McGrath

Visual Basic

in easy steps

In easy steps is an imprint of In Easy Steps Limited
Southfield Road · Southam
Warwickshire CV47 0FB · United Kingdom
www.ineasysteps.com

Second Edition

Notice of Liability
Every effort has been made to ensure that this book contains accurate
and current information. However, In Easy Steps Limited and the
author shall not be liable for any loss or damage suffered by readers
as a result of any information contained herein.

Trademarks
All trademarks are acknowledged as belonging to their respective
companies.

Printed and bound in the United Kingdom

ISBN-13 978-1-84078-358-2
ISBN-10 1-84078-358-3

Contents

Foreword

The examples in this book have been carefully prepared to demonstrate the many features of Visual Basic. You are encouraged to try out the examples on your own computer to discover the exciting possibilities offered by the Visual Basic programming language. The straightforward descriptions should enable you to easily recreate the examples manually or, if you prefer, you can download an archive containing all the example projects by following these simple steps:

1 Open your web browser and visit our website at **http://www.ineasysteps.com**

2 Navigate to the "Resource Center" and choose the "Downloads" section

3 Find the "From Visual Basic in easy steps, 2nd Edition" item in the "Source Code" list then click on the hyperlink entitled "Projects" to download the compressed ZIP archive

4 Extract the contents of the ZIP file to any convenient location on your computer – for easy reference these are arranged in sub-folders whose names match each chapter title of this book and each project is named as described in the book. For example, the "GettingStarted" project in the first chapter is located in the "1-Getting started" folder

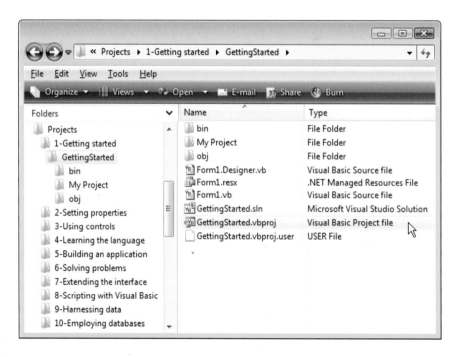

5 Double-click on the Visual Basic project file (file extension ".vbproj") in any project folder to launch that example in a Visual Basic Integrated Development Environment

1 Getting started

Welcome to the exciting world of Visual Basic programming. This chapter introduces the Visual Basic Integrated Development Environment (IDE) and shows you how to create a real Windows application.

Introduction

In choosing to start programming with Visual Basic you have made an excellent choice – the Visual Basic programming language offers the easiest way to write programs for Windows. This means you can easily create your own programs to give maximum control over your computer and automate your work to be more productive. Also, programming with Visual Basic is fun!

Like other programming languages Visual Basic comprises a number of significant "keywords" and a set of syntax rules. Beginners often find its syntax simpler than other programming languages making Visual Basic a popular first choice to learn.

Although writing programs can be complex Visual Basic makes it easy to get started. You can choose how far to go. Another advantage of Visual Basic is that it works with Microsoft Office and on the Internet – so the possibilities are immense...

- Visual Basic (VB) – quite simply the best programming language for the novice or hobbyist to begin creating their own standalone Windows applications, fast

- Visual Basic for Applications (VBA) – an implementation of Visual Basic that is built into all Microsoft Office applications. It runs within a host rather than as a standalone application

- Visual Basic Script (VBScript) – a derivative of Visual Basic that can be used for Windows scripting and client-side web page scripting for Internet Explorer

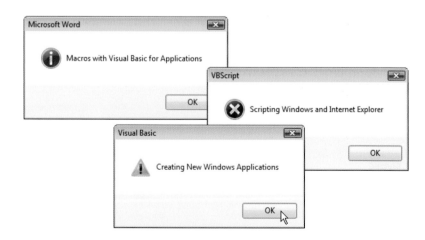

The evolution of Visual Basic

● Visual Basic 1.0 released in May 1991 at the Comdex trade show in Atlanta, Georgia, USA

● Visual Basic 2.0 released in November 1992 – introducing an easier and faster programming environment

● Visual Basic 3.0 released in the summer of 1993 – introducing the Microsoft Jet Database Engine for database programs

● Visual Basic 4.0 released in August 1995 – introducing support for controls based on the Component Object Model (COM)

● Visual Basic 5.0 released in February 1997 – introducing the ability to create custom user controls

● Visual Basic 6.0 released in the summer of 1998 – introducing the ability to create web-based programs. This hugely popular edition is the final version based on COM and is often referred to today as "Classic Visual Basic"

● Visual Basic 7.0 (also known as Visual Basic .NET) released in 2002 – introducing a very different object-oriented language based upon the Microsoft .NET framework. This controversial edition broke backward-compatability with previous versions and caused a rift within the developer community

● Visual Basic 8.0 (also known as Visual Basic 2005) – adding .NET 2.0 language features to the previous edition

● Visual Basic 9.0 (also known as Visual Basic 2008) – adding more powerful language features from the .NET 3.5 framework to the previous edition

All examples in this book have been created for Visual Basic 9.0 although many of the core language features are common to previous versions of the Visual Basic programming language.

Hot tip

Visual Basic derives from an earlier simple language called BASIC – Beginners All-purpose Symbolic Instruction Code. The "Visual" part was added later as many tasks can now be accomplished visually, without writing code.

9

Microsoft®
.net™

Installing Visual Basic

In order to create Windows applications with the Visual Basic programming language you will first need to install a Visual Basic Integrated Development Environment (IDE).

Microsoft Visual Studio is the professional development tool that provides a fully Integrated Development Environment for Visual C++, Visual C#, Visual J#, and Visual Basic. Within its IDE, code can be written in C++, C#, J# or the Visual Basic programming language to create Windows applications.

Microsoft Visual Basic Express Edition is a streamlined version of Visual Studio specially created for those people learning Visual Basic. It has a simplified user interface and omits advanced features of the professional edition to avoid confusion. Within its IDE, code can be written in the Visual Basic programming language to create Windows applications.

Both Visual Studio and Visual Basic Express Edition provide a Visual Basic IDE for Visual Basic programming. Unlike the fully-featured Visual Studio product, the Visual Basic Express Edition is completely free and can be installed on any system meeting the following minimum requirements:

Component	Requirement
Operating system	Windows® XP Windows Server 2003™ Windows Vista™ Windows Server 2008™
CPU (processor)	600 MHz minimum (1 GHz recommended)
RAM (memory)	192 Mb minimum (256 Mb recommended)
HDD (hard drive)	Up to 1.3 Gb of available space may be required

The Visual Basic Express Edition is used throughout this book to demonstrate programming with the Visual Basic language but the examples can also be recreated in Visual Studio. Follow the steps opposite to install Visual Basic Express Edition.

1 Open your web browser and navigate to the Visual Basic Express Edition download page on the Microsoft website – at the time of writing this can be found at **http://www.microsoft.com/express/download**

2 Click the Visual Basic Express Edition "Download" option then click "Run" in the File Download dialog that appears to run "vbsetup.exe"

3 When the "Welcome to Setup" dialog appears you may, optionally, check a box to allow information to be submitted to Microsoft. Click on the Next button to start the installation process

4 In the "License Terms" dialog you may, optionally, check a box to receive and display developer news via an online RSS feed. Click the button to agree the license terms, then click on Next to continue

5 Accept the suggested destination folder, then click on Install to complete the installation of both Visual Basic and the bundled SQL Server database software

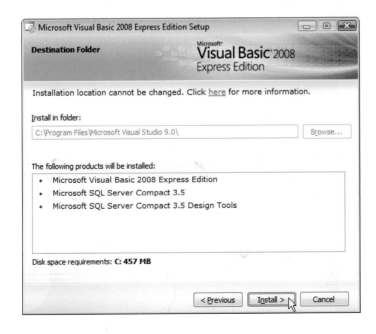

> **Hot tip**
>
> Installation may also offer to install the Microsoft Silverlight Runtime for Internet Explorer. You may choose to do so but this is not required for Visual Basic.

> **Beware**
>
> Choosing a different destination folder may require other paths to be adjusted later – it's simpler to just accept the suggested default.

11

Exploring the IDE

To launch the Visual Basic Integrated Development Environment click Start, All Programs, then select the Visual Basic menu item:

Almost immediately the Visual Basic Integrated Development Environment (IDE) appears from which you have instant access to everything needed to produce complete Windows applications – from here you can create exciting visual interfaces, enter code, compile and execute applications, debug errors, and much more.

The Visual Basic IDE initially includes a default Start Page, along with the standard IDE components, and looks like this:

Menu
Bar

Tool
Bar

Toolbox

Recent
Projects

Getting
Started

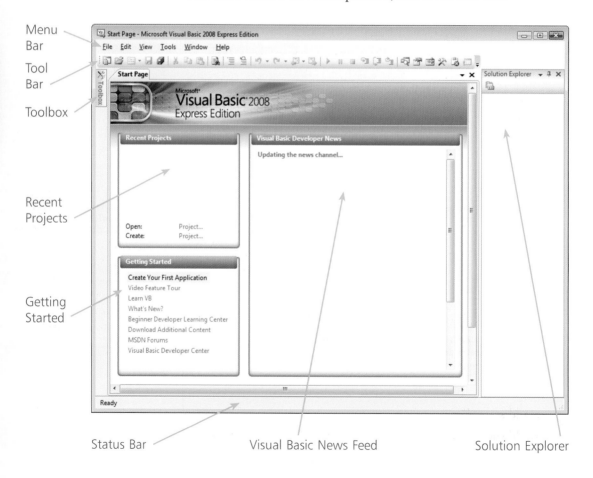

Status Bar   Visual Basic News Feed   Solution Explorer

Start Page elements

The default start page provides these useful features:

- **Recent Projects** – conveniently lists recently opened projects so you can select one to reopen, or create a brand new project

- **Getting Started** – contains helpful hyperlinks offering assistance on Visual Basic topics

- **Visual Basic Developer News** – feeds the latest online news direct from the Microsoft Developer Network (MSDN)

Visual Basic IDE components

The Viual Basic IDE initially provides these standard features:

- **Menu Bar** – where you can select actions to perform on all your project files and to access Help. When a project is open extra menus of Project, Build, Debug, and Data, are shown in addition to the default menu selection of File, Edit, View, Tools, Window, and Help

- **Tool Bar** – where you can perform the most popular menu actions with just a single click on its associated shortcut icon

- **Toolbox** – where you can select visual elements to add to a project. Place the cursor over the Toolbox to see its contents. When a project is open "controls", such as Button, Label, CheckBox, RadioButton, and TextBox, are shown here

- **Solution Explorer** – where you can see at a glance all the files and resource components contained within an open project

- **Status Bar** – where you can read the state of the current activity being undertaken. When building an application a "Build started" message is displayed here, changing to a "Build succeeded" or "Build failed" message upon completion

13

Starting a new project

1 On the Menu Bar click File, New Project, or press the Ctrl+N keys, to open the New Project dialog box

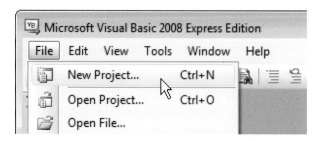

2 In the New Project dialog box select the Windows Forms Application template icon

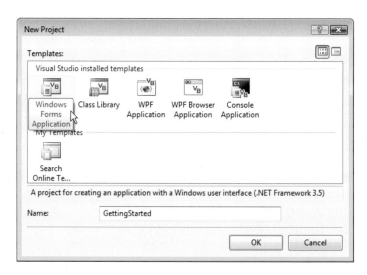

Hot tip

The New Project dialog automatically selects the Windows Forms Application template by default as it is the most often used template.

3 Enter a project name of your choice in the Name field then click on the OK button to create the new project – in this case the project name will be "GettingStarted"

Visual Basic now creates your new project and loads it into the IDE. A new tabbed Form Designer window appears (over the Start Page tabbed window) displaying a default Form and a Properties window is added below the Solution Explorer.

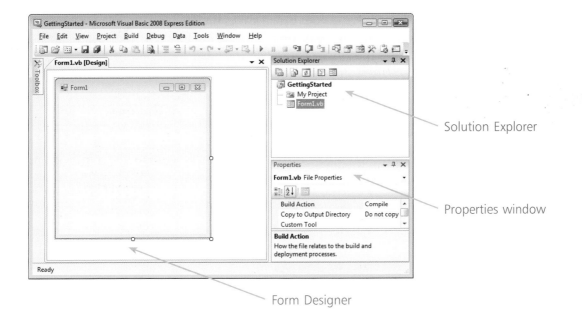

Solution Explorer

Properties window

Form Designer

The Form Designer is where you create visual interfaces for your applications and the Properties window contains details of the item that is currently selected in the Form Designer window.

The Visual Basic IDE has now gathered all the resources needed to build a default Windows application – click the Start Debugging button on the Tool Bar to launch this application.

Start Debugging

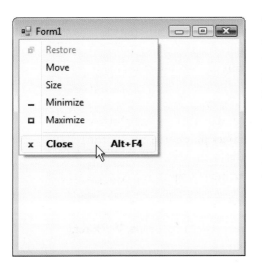

The application simply creates a basic window – you can move it, minimize it, maximize it, resize it, and quit the application by closing it. It may not do much but you have already created a real Windows program!

Hot tip

You can alternatively run applications using the F5 keyboard shortcut key.

15

Adding a visual control

The Toolbox in the Visual Basic IDE contains a wide range of visual controls which are the building blocks of your applications. Using the project created on the previous page follow these steps to start using the Toolbox now:

1 Place the cursor over the vertical Toolbox tab at the left edge of the IDE window, or click View, Toolbox on the Menu Bar, to display the Toolbox contents. The visual controls are contained under various category headings beside a "+" expansion button

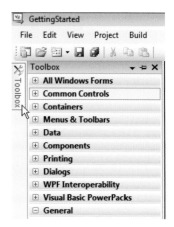

2 Click on the "+" button beside the Common Controls category heading to expand the list of most commonly used visual controls. Usefully each control name appears beside an icon depicting that control as a reminder. You can click on the category button again, to collapsse the list, then expand the other categories to explore the range of controls available to build your application interfaces

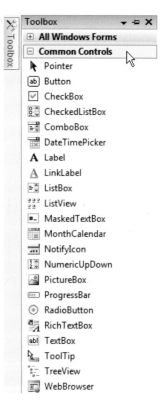

3 Click'n'drag the Button item from the Common Controls category in the Toolbox onto the Form in the Designer window, or double-click the Button item, to add a Button control to the Form

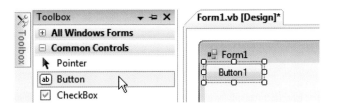

The Button control appears in the Form Designer surrounded by "handles" which can be dragged to resize the button's width and height. Click the Start Debugging button, or press F5, to run the application and try out your button.

The Button control behaves in a familiar Windows application manner with "states" that visually react to the cursor:

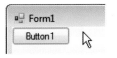

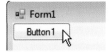

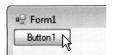

Default State   Hover State   Down State

Adding functional code

The Visual Basic IDE automatically generates code, in the background, to incorporate the visual controls you add to your program interface. Additional code can be added manually, using the IDE's integral Code Editor, to determine how your program should respond to interface events – such as when the user clicks a button.

Using the project created on the previous page follow these steps to start using the Visual Basic Code Editor now:

1 Double-click on the Button control you have added to the default Form in the Designer window. A new tabbed text window opens in the IDE – this is the Code Editor window

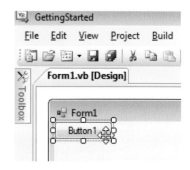

2 The cursor is automatically placed at precisely the right point in the code at which to add an instruction to determine what the program should do when this button is clicked. Type the instruction **MsgBox("Hello World!")** so the Code Editor looks exactly like this:

Hot tip

Switch easily between the Code Editor and Form Designer (or Start Page) by clicking on the appropriate window tab.

...cont'd

3 Click the Start Debugging button, or press F5, to run the application and test the code you have just written to handle the event that occurs when the button is clicked

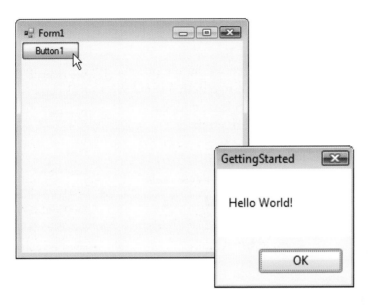

4 Push the OK button to close the dialog box, then click the "X" button on the Form window, or click the Stop Debugging button on the Menu Bar, to stop the program

Each time the button in this application is pressed the program reads the line of code you added manually to produce a dialog box containing the specified message. The action of pressing the button creates a "Click" event that refers to the associated "event-handler" section of code you added to see how to respond.

In fact most Windows software works by responding to events in this way. For instance, when you press a key in a word processor a character appears in the document – the "KeyPress" event calls upon its event-handler code to update the text in response.

The process of providing intelligent responses to events in your programs is the very cornerstone of creating Windows applications with Visual Basic.

Saving projects

Even the simplest Visual Basic project comprises multiple files which must each be saved on your system to store the project.

Follow these steps to save the current New Project to disk:

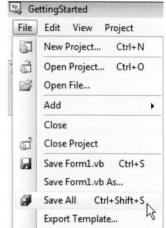
1 Click the Save All button on the Tool Bar, or click File, Save All on the Menu Bar, or press the Ctr+Shift+S keys, to open the Save Project dialog

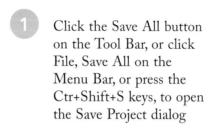

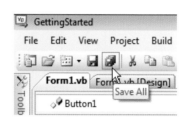

2 In the Save Project dialog you can optionally change the Project name if it is part of a larger Solution – for simple applications just leave the Project name the same as the Solution Name

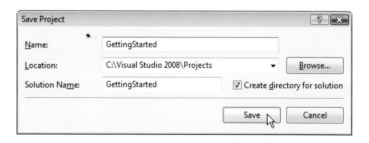

3 Choose a Location at which to save your project, or accept the suggested Location

4 Ensure that the "Create directory..." box is checked, then click the Save button to save all your project files

Reopening projects

Use these steps to re-open a saved Visual Basic project:

1 Click File, Open Project on the Menu Bar, or press the Ctrl+O keys, to launch the Open Project dialog

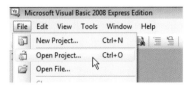

2 In the Open Project dialog navigate to the location at which you saved your project

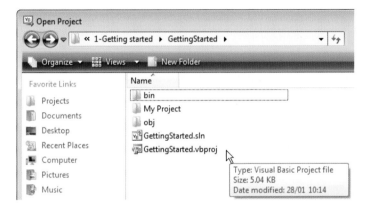

3 Double-click on either the Visual Basic Project File with the extension ".vbproj", or the Visual Basic Solution file with the extension ".sln", to open the project in the IDE

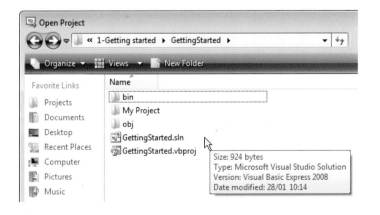

Beware

Only have one project open at any given time to avoid confusion – unless several are needed to be open together for advanced programming.

Hot tip

If you don't see the Form Designer window after reopening a project click the Form1.vb icon in Solution Explorer to make it appear.

Summary

- The Windows Application Template in the New Project dialog is used to begin creating a new Windows application project

- A unique name should be entered into the New Project dialog whenever you create a new Visual Basic project

- The Form Designer window of the Visual Basic IDE is where you create the visual interface for your program

- Visual controls are added from the Toolbox to create the interface layout you want for your program

- A control can be dragged from the Toolbox and dropped onto the Form, or added to the Form with a double-click

- The Visual Basic IDE automatically generates code in the background as you develop your program visually

- The Code Editor window of the Visual Basic IDE is where you manually add extra code to your program

- Double-click on any control in the Form designer to open the Code Editor window at that control's event-handler code

- The Start Debugging button on the Visual Basic Tool Bar can be used to run the current project application

- Pressing a button control in a running application creates a Click event within the program

- Code added to a button's Click event-handler determines how your program will respond whenever its Click event occurs

- Providing intelligent responses to events in your programs is the cornerstone of programming with Visual Basic

- Remember to explicitly save your working project using the Save All button on the Tool Bar to avoid accidental loss

- Select the project file with the ".vbproj" or ".sln" extension in your chosen saved project directory to re-open that project

2 Setting properties

This chapter describes how properties of an application can be changed at "designtime", when you are creating the interface, and at "runtime", when the application is actually in use.

Form properties

Most applications created with Visual Basic are based upon a window Form – a canvas on which to paint the user interface. In some cases an application will have more than one Form and Visual Basic lets you display and hide Forms while the application is running. Closing the main Form quits the application.

Like all Visual Basic objects, each Form has several interesting familiar properties, such as those distinguished below.

Icon – a small graphic appearing at the top left corner of the open Form, and when it's minimized

Text – a caption appearing in the title bar of the open Form, and when it's minimized

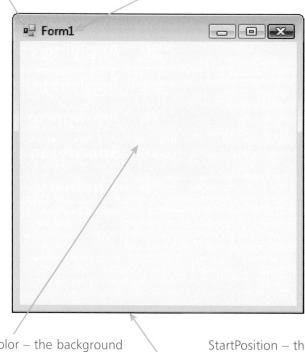

BackColor – the background color of the Form

StartPosition – the initial location of the Form on the Windows desktop

Size – the height and width of the Form

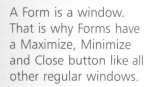

Don't forget

A Form is a window. That is why Forms have a Maximize, Minimize and Close button like all other regular windows.

24

Meeting the property editor

The Visual Basic IDE provides a Properties window where object properties can be inspected. This displays a list of the currently selected object's properties, along with their present values. The full list of Form properties, for example, is much larger than the few shown opposite and can be inspected in the property editor.

1 Identify the Properties window in the IDE – if it's not visible click View, Properties Window, or press the F4 key, to open it

2 Click on File, New Project to start a new Windows application using the suggested default name

3 Click on the blank Form in the Form Designer window to display its properties in the Properties window

4 Try out the Properties window buttons, immediately above the property list, to explore different types of Categorical and Alphabetical display

5 Use the scroll bar in the Properties window to examine the complete list of Form properties and their present values

Editing property values

Changing the properties of a Visual Basic object allows you to determine the appearance of that object. When creating an interface, at designtime, an object's Size property can be changed by moving its handles to resize it in the Form Designer window – its new dimension values will then appear in the Properties window. More usefully, the value of each single Form and Control property can be edited directly in the Properties window.

Editing a Form property value

1 Click on a default blank Form in the Form Designer window to display its properties in the Properties window

2 Find the Text property in the Properties window then double-click in the value column alongside it to highlight the present value – this will be "Form1" by default

3 Type "New Caption" to specify that as a new value for the Text property – the text string appears in the value column as you type

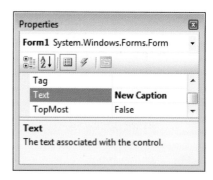

4 Hit Return, or click anywhere else, to apply the new value – it now also appears on the Form in the Form Designer

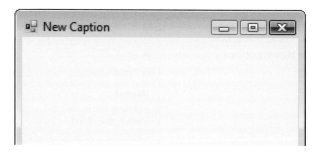

Beware

Although a new value has been assigned to the Form's Text property here its (Name) property still has the default value of "Form1" for reference in Visual Basic programming code.

Editing a Control property value

1 Click View, Toolbox on the Menu Bar or press Ctrl+Alt+X, to open the ToolBox

2 Click'n'drag the Label item from the Common Controls category, or double-click on it, to add a Label control to a blank default Form

3 In the Form Designer window double-click on the Label control to display its present property values in the Properties window

4 Find the Text property in the Properties window then double-click in the value column alongside it to highlight the present value – this will be "Label1" by default

5 Type "New Label Text" to specify that as a new value for the Text property – the text string appears in the value column as you type

6 Hit Return, or click anywhere else, to apply the new value – it now also appears on the Label in the Form Designer

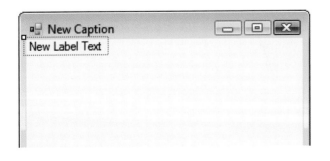

Hot tip

Some properties, such as Icon, provide a browse button when you click on their value column so you can navigate to the location of a local resource to select as the new property value.

27

Don't forget

Whenever you make changes in the IDE Visual Basic works in the background to make associated changes to the underlying code.

Coding property values

In addition to setting property design values for your application in the Properties window you may also set some text and color values in programming code, so the properties get assigned their initial values (are "initialized") when the Form first loads.

Statements to initialize property values should be placed within the Form's Load event-handler. This executes the statements it contains when it is called by the action of the Form loading – just as the Click event-handler executes its statements when it is called by the action of a user clicking the Button.

Initializing Control properties

1. Cick on File, New Project, or press Ctrl+N, to start a new Windows application and name it "Initialize"

2. Click'n'drag a Label item from the Common Controls category, or double-click on it, to add a Label control to a blank default Form

3. In the Form Designer window double-click anywhere on the default Form to launch the Code Editor – the cursor is automatically placed in the Form's Load event-handler section of code, ready to add statements

4. Type the instruction **Label1.BackColor = Color.Yellow** to set the Label's background to yellow, then hit Return

5. Type the instruction **Label1.Text = "Initialized Text"** to set the Label's text content, then hit Return

6. Click on the Start Debugging button, or press F5, to run the application and see that the Label properties initialize with the values you have specified

28

Initializing Form properties

1. Click the Stop Debugging button to halt the Initialize application and return once more to the Code Editor at the Form's Load event-handler section of code

2. Add the instruction **Form1.BackColor = Color.Blue** to attempt to set the Form's background to blue, then hit Return – notice that a blue wavy underline now appears beneath **Form1.BackColor** on this line of code

3. Place the mouse pointer over the blue wavy line and read the ToolTip message that pops up

```
Form1.BackColor = Color.Blue
```
'Initialize.Form1' cannot refer to itself through its default instance; use 'Me' instead.

4. The ToolTip message means you cannot refer to the Form by its name within its own event-handler, so change the instruction to **Me.BackColor = Color.Blue** – now hit Return and see the blue wavy underline disappear

5. Type the instruction **Me.Text = "Initialized Caption"** to set the Form's text caption, then hit Return

6. Click on the Start Debugging button, or press F5, to run the application and see that the Form properties initialize with the values you have specified

Don't forget

You need to hit the Return key after typing each statement so that only one statement appears on each line.

29

Beware

Use the special Me keyword in place of the Form's name if you want to address to the Form.

Applying computed values

The Properties window and initialization code technique allows the programmer to specify static property values at designtime. Creating code to calculate further values from known static values allows your application to compute property values at runtime.

1 Cick on File, New Project, or press Ctrl+N, to start a new Windows application and name it "Compute"

2 From the ToolBox add six Label controls and one Button control to the default Form, then drag them into position so the Form looks something like the arrangement below

3 Selecting each item in turn use the Properties window to change the Text property value of the Form, Button, and all Labels, to look like this

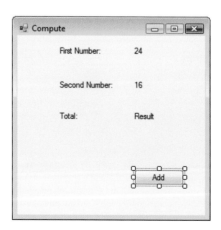

4 To avoid confusion with other controls use the Properties window to change the (Name) property of the three Labels down the right-hand side of the form to be **Num1**, **Num2**, and **Sum**, reading from top-to-bottom – the new names can now be used in Visual Basic programming code to refer to these controls

5 Double-click on the Button to open the Code Editor within its Click event-handler section of code. Here's where a statement can be added to calculate the total of the static Text property values of **Num1** and **Num2**.

6 Type **Sum.Text = Val(Num1.Text) + Val(Num2.Text)** then hit Return to add a statement assigning the computed total value to the Sum Label's Text property

7 Click on the Start Debugging button, or press F5, to run the application. Click the button to execute the statement you added and see the **Sum** total value appear

Don't forget

The Visual Basic Val() function is used here to extract the numeric version of the text string values so it can perform arithmetic on them – arithmetic functions are fully explained later.

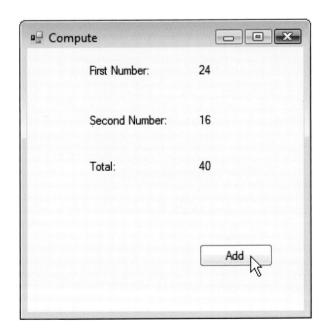

Compute

First Number: 24

Second Number: 16

Total: 40

Add

Hot tip

Try adding a further Button to provide a clear facility with the statement Sum.Text="" in its event-handler.

Applying user values

While the Label control works great to display an assigned Text property value it does not allow the user to directly input a value. The TextBox control does both and should be used instead of a Label control where direct dynamic user input is desirable.

Replacing the Label controls named **Num1** and **Num2** in the previous example with TextBox controls of the same name allows the user to dynamically change those values used to compute the Sum total value when the Button is clicked.

1 Cick on File, New Project, or press Ctrl+N, to start a new Windows application and name it "UserInput"

2 From the ToolBox add four Label controls, two TextBox controls, and two Button controls to the default Form

3 Use the Properties window to change the Text property value of the Form, Buttons, and Labels, and arrange their position so the interface looks something like this

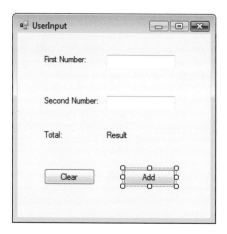

4 To avoid confusion with other controls use the Properties window to change the (Name) property of the two TextBox controls to **Num1** and **Num2**, the Button controls to **AddBtn** and **ClearBtn**, and the Label with the "Result" Text value to **Sum** – the new names can now be used in programming code to refer to these controls

5 Double-click on the **AddBtn** to open the Code Editor within its Click event-handler and add the statement **Sum.Text = Val(Num1.Text) + Val(Num2.Text)**.

6 Double-click on the **ClearBtn** to open the Code Editor within its Click event-handler and add the statements **Sum.Text = "Result" : Num1.Text = "" : Num2.Text = ""**.

7 Click on the Start Debugging button, or press F5, to run the application. Enter any numeric values you like into the TextBox fields then click the Add button to see the **Sum** total value

UserInput

First Number: 22.5

Second Number: 47.5

Total: 70

Clear   Add

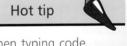

8 Click the Clear button to assign new property values, resuming the application's initial state and ready to add two more input values

Prompting for input

In addition to input via Form window controls, an application can seek user input from an InputBox dialog. This is similar to a MsgBox dialog but also has a text field where the user can type input that will be returned to the application. The user input value can then be assigned to a property in the usual way.

Unlike a simple code statement that calls up a MsgBox, just to advise the user, a statement that calls up an InputBox should make an assignation of the returned value.

1   Cick on File, New Project, or press Ctrl+N, to start a new Windows application and name it "DialogInput"

2   From the ToolBox add a Button control to the Form

3   Double-click on the Button to open the Code Editor within its Click event-handler and add the statement
Me.Text = InputBox("Enter a Caption...")

4   Click the Start Debugging button, or press F5, to run the application then click the Button to call up the InputBox

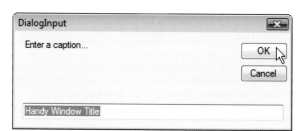

5   Enter any text you like into the input field then click the OK button to assign the value of your input to the Form's Text property as a window title caption

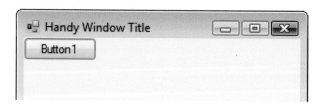

InputBox Title and Default Response

Notice that the InputBox title caption assumes the name of the application by default – in this case it's "DialogInput". You may, however, specify your own InputBox title by adding a second string after the message string within the parentheses.

Optionally, you may specify a default response that will appear in the text field when the InputBox is called by adding a third string within the parentheses. All strings must be separated by a comma.

Notice how the special space+underscore characters are used here to allow the statement to continue on the next line.

1. In the DialogInput application double-click on the Button to reopen the Code Editor within its Click event-handler and edit the previous statement to read
Me.Text = InputBox("Enter a Caption..." , _
"Caption Selecter" , "Dandy Window Title")

2. Click the Start Debugging button, or press F5, to run the application then click the Button to call up the InputBox

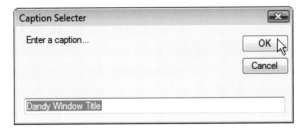

Hot tip

3. Note the InputBox title caption, then click the OK button to assign the default response value to the Form's Text property as a window title caption

Try specifying a message and a default response – separating the two strings by TWO commas.

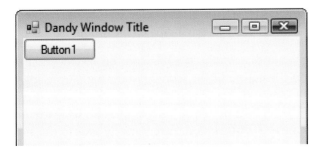

Specifying dialog properties

The features of a MsgBox dialog can be determined by adding a comma and specification value after the message string within its parentheses. This can specify which buttons the dialog will display and what graphic icon, if any, will appear on the dialog.

Button constant	Value
vbOkOnly	0
vbOkCancel	1
vbAbortRetryIgnore	2
vbYesNoCancel	3
vbYesNo	4
vbRetryCancel	5

The dialog button combinations can be specified using the Visual Basic constant values, or their numeric equivalents, in this table. For example, to have the dialog display Yes, No, and Cancel buttons specify the **vbYesNoCancel** constant or its numeric equivalent **3**.

Icon constant		Value
vbCritical	❌	16
vbQuestion	❓	32
vbExclamation	⚠	48
vbInformation	ℹ	64

The dialog icon can be specified using the Visual Basic constant values, or their numeric equivalents, in this table. For example, to have the dialog display the question mark icon specify the **vbQuestion** constant or its numeric equivalent **32**.

Hot tip

Always specify a graphic icon when calling a MsgBox dialog to help the user easily understand the nature of the message.

In order to have the MsgBox display both a particular button combination and a certain graphic icon the specification can add the button constant and the icon constant together using the addition + operator. For example, the specification to display Yes, No, and Cancel buttons along with a question icon would be **vbYesNoCancel + VbQuestion**. Alternatively specify the sum total of their numeric equivalents – in this case it's **35** (3 + 32).

The buttons in a MsgBox dialog each return a specific numeric value to the application when they are clicked. This can be assigned to a property in much the same way as the value returned from the InputBox dialog in the previous example.

1. Cick on File, New Project, or press Ctrl+N, to start a new Windows application and name it "MsgBoxDialog"

2. From the ToolBox add a Button, a Label, and a TextBox to the default Form and arrange them to your liking

3. Set the Label's Text property to "Button Value :" and name the TextBox **BtnValue**

4. Double-click on the Button to open the Code Editor within its Click event-handler and add the statement
BtnValue.Text = MsgBox("Click any button" , _ vbYesNoCancel + vbQuestion)

5. Like it says, click any button, then note the value it has returned to the TextBox

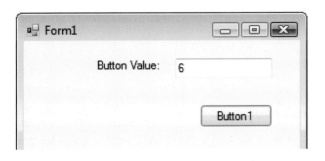

37

Summary

- In Visual Basic each object has a name and properties

- When an object is selected in the Form Designer the current value of each of its properties can be inspected in the Properties window

- The value of any property can be edited in the Properties window to assign a new value to that property

- Features determining the appearance of an application, such as Font and Layout, can be set at designtime along with content

- Content, such as Text and Color values, can also be initialized at runtime using the Form's Load event-handler

- Control objects placed on a Form can be addressed by their name but you should use the Me keyword to address the current Form itself

- Programming code can use existing property values in a calculation to compute a further value at runtime

- Label controls merely display text, they do not allow user input

- TextBox controls both display text and allow user input

- It is recommended you give all controls a meaningful name for easy recognition

- Visual Basic is not case-sensitive so no special care is needed to observe capital or lower case letters in code

- An InputBox allows user input to be assigned to any property

- Unlike a MsgBox statement, a call to the InputBox should always assign the value which will be returned

- Optionally, a title and default response can be specified for an InputBox dialog

- Optionally, a button combination and icon can be specified for a MsgBox dialog

3 Using controls

This chapter illustrates how many of the Common Controls within the Visual Basic Toolbox can be used to develop an exciting application interface.

Tab order

When creating an application interface with multiple controls consider how it can be navigated without a mouse, by those users who prefer keyboard navigation. Typically they will expect to be able to move the focus from one control to another by pressing the Tab key. It is, therefore, important to allow the focus to move in a logical order when the Tab key is pressed, by setting the TabIndex property values of your controls.

Hot tip

In Windows applications the term "focus" describes which control is active. Pressing the Enter key is equivalent to clicking on the control in current focus.

1 Place several controls on a Form then click on the one you want to be first in the tab order to select it

2 Set the TabIndex property value of the selected control to zero so it has first focus

Don't forget

Not all controls can receive focus. The Label controls in this example are not able to get focus so the tab action just skips to the next control.

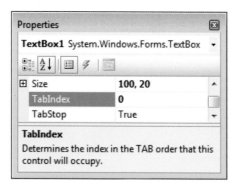

3 Repeat for other controls setting each TabIndex with an ascending value – 1, 2, 3, and so on

Using Button

The Button control provides the user with an easy way to start an operation, confirm or cancel a choice, or get help. In Visual Basic, programming code needs to be added within each Button's event-handler to determine its function. Also its properties need to be set to determine its appearance – Size, Text, Color, Font, etc. When setting the Text property you can easily create an access key shortcut by prefixing the value with an ampersand & character.

Hot tip

The Enabled property can be set to False to prevent a Button being available to the user until your program enables it.

1 Select the Button control in the Form Designer then use the Properties window to modify its Size, and Color

![KeyboardNavigation form with Label1, Label2, Stop and Go buttons]

2 Assign a Text property value that is prefixed by an ampersand & character to create an access key shortcut

Beware

The standard Windows look is familiar and comfortable for most users – avoid radical customization of your application.

![Properties window showing GoBtn System.Windows.Forms.Button, with Text property set to &Go]

Properties

GoBtn System.Windows.Forms.Button

TabStop	True
Tag	
Text	&Go
TextAlign	MiddleCenter
TextImageRelation	Overlay

Text
The text associated with the control.

3 Repeat for other Button controls, setting each Text property with a unique access key shortcut value, then press Alt+G to test this "Go" button's access key

Using TextBox

The TextBox control is an essential part of most applications, typically providing a single-line text input area for the user. Greater amounts of text input can be accommodated in a TextBox if its Multiline property is set to True and its ScrollBars property is set to Vertical.

1 Place a TextBox and a Button control onto a Form

2 Select the TextBox and use the Properties window to set its ScrollBars property to Vertical

3 Click on the Smart Tag arrowed button over the TextBox., or use the Properties window, to set its Multiline property to True

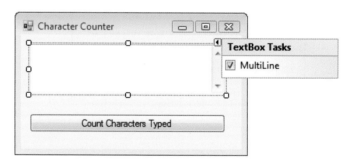

Hot tip

The ampersand & character is used in this example to concatenate (join) the code together.

4 Add this statement to the Button's Click event-handler
MsgBox("You typed: " & _
Str (Len (TextBox1.Text)) & " characters")

5 Run the application, type some text into the TextBox, then click the Button to test the application

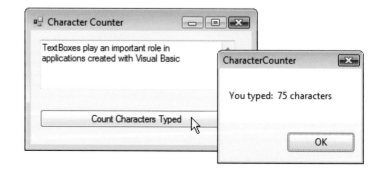

Using ComboBox

A ComboBox control can be used in place of a TextBox to provide an additional range of text values in a dropdown list. The user can choose one of the listed values to insert into the text field or type into it directly, just like a regular TextBox. The ComboBox provides a user-friendly list of anticipated input but occupies only the same space as a single-line TextBox.

1 Select the ComboBox control and find its Items property in the Properties window

2 Click the ellipsis (...) button in its value column to launch the String Collection editor

3 Enter a list of alternatives you wish to offer, adding one on each line, then click the OK button

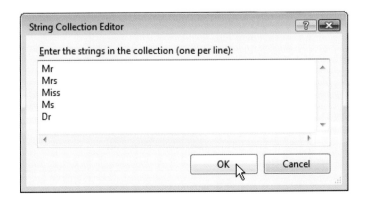

Don't forget

You can discover the value selected by the user from the ComboBox's Text property.

43

Using Label

A Label control is intended to advise the user and provides a rectangular area that is generally used to provide text information. It can also provide simple rectangular graphics by displaying no text value and setting its AutoSize and BackColor properties.

Hot tip

You can add an outline to a Label using its BorderStyle property.

1 Add three Label controls to a Form

2 Select each Label in turn and, in the Properties window, set the AutoSize property value to False

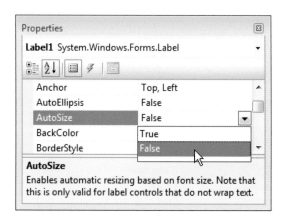

3 Select each Label in turn and, in the Properties window, set the BackColor property value to your preference

Don't forget

You can use the dropdown list in the Properties window to select a control to edit.

4 Select each Label in turn and, in the Properties window, delete the Text property value so it becomes blank

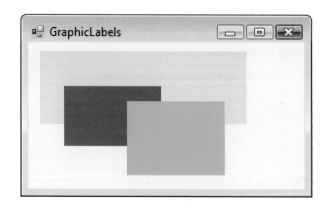

44

Using PictureBox

The PictureBox control allows images to be added to your application interface. These can be referenced as local files or imported into your application as a resource. Adding an image as a resource ensures your application will be portable when deployed as it includes its own copy of the image.

1 Add a PictureBox control to a Form then select it

2 Find its Image property in the Properties window then click the ellipsis button [...] to launch the Select Resource dialog box

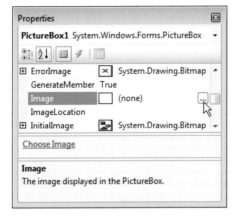

3 Click the "Project resource file" radio button then click Import to browse to the location of the image file

4 Click OK to import the image file into your application and to place the image in the PictureBox control

Beware

Acceptable image formats are Bitmap (.bmp), Icon (.ico), GIF (.gif), Metafile (.wmf), and JPEG (.jpg) – other formats cannot be imported unless they are converted first.

45

Hot tip

Notice after importing an image how the file gets added into the Resources folder in the Solution Explorer window.

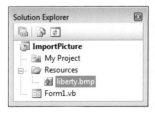

Using ListBox

The Visual Basic ListBox is one of the most useful controls as it provides a convenient way to present multiple choices to the user. It allows large lists, of even several thousand items, to be displayed in a compact manner. Typically the list data is derived from an external source, such as a database, then incorporated within your application – address books, business records, collections, etc.

Although the Properties window allows items to be added manually to a ListBox Items property, as with a ComboBox, it is often more appropriate to build the list dynamically by adding items at runtime – using the Form's Load evnt-handler.

Hot tip

You don't need to worry about setting ListBox scroll bars for longer lists – they get added automatically.

1 Add a ListBox, Label, and Button control to a Form

2 Name the ListBox "BookList" and change the Text property values of the Label and Button like this

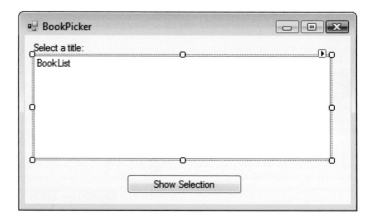

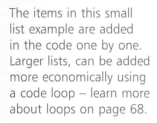

Don't forget

The items in this small list example are added in the code one by one. Larger lists, can be added more economically using a code loop – learn more about loops on page 68.

3 Double-click on the Form to open the Code Editor in the Form's Load event-handler and add the statement **BookList.Items.Add("HTML in easy steps")**

4 Repeat the above statement, each on a new line, substituting a different title within the parentheses for each title you want to add to the list

5 To have the list items sorted alphabetically add the statement **BookList.Sorted = True**

6 To have the first item in the list selected by default add the statement **BookList.SelectedIndex = 0**

7 To show the list length in the Form caption add the statement **Me.Text = BookList.Items.Count & _
" More Books by Mike McGrath"**

8 Return to the Form Designer and double-click on the Button to open the Code Editor in its event-handler. To display the current selected list item when it is clicked add the statement **MsgBox(BookList.Text)**

Beware

Remember that the first item in the index is numbered as zero, not 1.

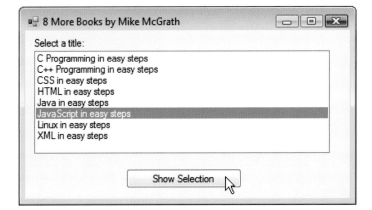

9 Run the application and see the first item appear selected. Select a different item then click the Button to confirm the selection

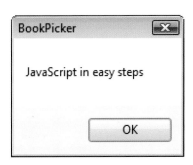

Hot tip

The ListBox's Sorted property can also be set in the Properties window.

47

Using CheckBox

A CheckBox control is a small box with a caption. It lets the user select the caption choice by clicking on the box and a check mark appears in the box to indicate it has been chosen. Clicking the box once more deselects the choice and unchecks the box.

CheckBox controls are ideal to present a set of choices from which the user can select none, one, or more than one choice.

1 Add two CheckBox controls to a Form along with a Label, ListBox, and Button

2 Use the Properties window to change the Text property values of the CheckBox controls, Label, and Button to look like the ones below and name the ListBox "Pizza"

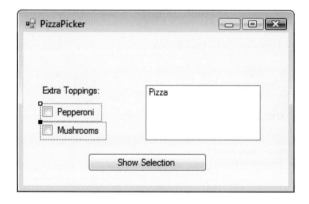

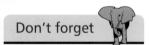
3 Add this statement to the Button's Click event-handler to clear the list box when it's clicked **Pizza.Items.Clear()**

4 Now add these statements to add list items for each checked CheckBox control
```
If CheckBox1.Checked = True Then
        Pizza.Items.Add( Checkbox1.Text )
End If

If CheckBox2.Checked = True Then
        Pizza.Items.Add( Checkbox2.Text )
End If
```

Using RadioButton

A RadioButton control is like a CheckBox, but with one crucial difference – the user can check only one choice in the group. Checking a RadioButton automatically unchecks any others.

RadioButton controls are ideal to present a set of choices from which the user can select only one choice.

1 Add two RadioButtons and a Label to the Form opposite then edit their Text properties so they look like this

2 Insert these statements in the Button's Click event-handler right after the clear instruction

```
If RadioButton1.Checked = True Then
        Pizza.Items.Add( RadioButton1.Text )
End If

If RadioButton2.Checked = True Then
        Pizza.Items.Add( RadioButton2.Text )
End If
```

3 Run the application, select various choices, then click the Button to test the selection results

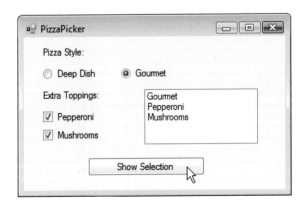

Using WebBrowser

The Visual Basic WebBrowser control makes it a snap to quickly add a document viewer to your application that can view HTML documents both online and on your own computer. It can also display plain text and image files – just like Internet Explorer.

1 Add a WebBrowser control to a Form – it will automatically occupy the entire Form area

2 Click on the Smart Tag arrow button and select the link to "Undock in parent container"

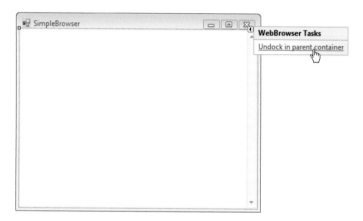

3 Add a TextBox and Button control then arrange the Form controls to look like this

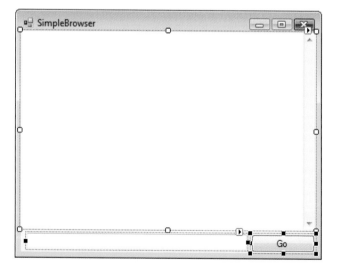

4 Double-click on the Button to open the Code Editor in its event-handler then add the following statement
WebBrowser1.Navigate(TextBox1.Text)

5 Run the application, type a valid URL into the TextBox field, then click the Button to view the web page

Beware

The Enter key will not activate the Button's click event unless you add an access key shortcut.

6 Now type a valid local file address into the TextBox field and click the Button to view it in the WebBrowser

Hot tip

You can download the projects from this book at www.ineasysteps.com.

Using Timer

The Timer is an invisible control that can be found in the Components section of the Visual Basic ToolBox. When added to your application it fires an event at a regular interval set by you. Statements within the Timer's event-handler are then executed whenever the Timer event occurs.

Hot tip

Set the PictureBox controls to AutoSize using the Smart Tags or the Properties window.

1 Add two PictureBox controls and a Button to a Form

2 Assign two similar images of the same size to the PictureBox controls then hold down the Shift key while you click on each to select both together

3 On the Menu Bar select Format, Align, Centers to exactly align the PictureBox controls one above the other

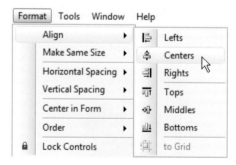

Beware

Controls can be accidentally repositioned – use Lock Controls under the Format menu to be sure they stay put.

4 Select Format, Order, Bring to Front or Send to Back to ensure that PictureBox1 is at the front (on top) of the PictureBox2 control – click on the top one and check the current selected control name in the Properties window

5 Add a Timer control to the Form from the Components section of the ToolBox – its icon appears on the Component Tray at the bottom of the Form Designer

6 Double-click on the Timer icon to open the Code Editor at its event-handler then add these statements

```
If PictureBox1.Visible = True Then
        PictureBox1.Visible = False
Else
        PictureBox1.Visible = True
End If
```

This code inspects the Visible property of the top PictureBox and "toggles" its visibility on and off – like flicking a light switch

7 Double-click on the Button to open the Code Editor at its event-handler then add these statements

```
If Timer1.Enabled = False Then
        Timer1.Enabled = True
Else
        Timer1.Enabled = False
End If
```

This code inspects the Enabled property of the Timer and "toggles" it on and off when the Button gets clicked

8 Run the application then click the Button to watch the Timer appear to animate the PictureBox images

Summary

- The TabIndex property determines the order in which a user can navigate around the interface controls with the Tab key

- Access key shortcuts are assigned to Buttons by prefixing the Text property value with an ampersand & character

- TextBox controls can usefully display multiple lines of text if their MultiLine property is set to True and their ScrollBars property is set to Vertical

- A ComboBox control allows typed text input, like a TextBox, plus it offers the user a list of anticipated input items to click

- Label controls contain text information and do not allow focus or direct input. They can, however, be useful to provide simple rectangular graphics

- A PictureBox control allows an image to be incorporated in the application interface

- Importing images as a resource ensure that the application will be portable when it is deployed

- ListBox controls are useful to compactly display numerous data items – both from within the program and from external sources such as a database

- CheckBox controls let the user choose none, one, or more options, whereas RadioButton controls let the user choose just one option from a group

- A WebBrowser control can display HTML documents plus plain text and images – just like your regular web browser

- You can use a Timer control to create an event in your application that fires at a regular interval set by you

- The toggle technique is useful in Visual Basic programming to alternate a Property value

4 Learning the language

This chapter demonstrates the mechanics of the Visual Basic programming language which allow data to be stored, controlled, and manipulated, to progress the application.

Elements of a program

A program is simply a series on instructions that tell the computer what to do. Although programs can be complex each individual instruction is generally simple. The computer starts at the beginning and works through, line by line, until it gets to the end. Here are some of the essential elements in Visual Basic:

Statements

A statement is an instruction that performs an action. For example, the statement **Lbl.BackColor = Color.Blue** sets the background color of **Lbl** to **Blue**.

Functions

A function is a statement that returns a value. For example, the function **InputBox()** returns the value of its dialog text field.

Variables

A variable is a word defined in the program that stores a value. For example, the statement **msg = "Hello World!"** stores a string of characters in a variable called **msg**.

Operators

An operator is an arithmetical symbol. For example, the * asterisk character is the multiplication operator and the / forward slash character is the division operator.

Objects

An object is a program "building block" entity. It can be visible, like a Button control, or invisible like a Timer control.

Properties

A property is a characteristic of an object. For example, the property **Btn.Text** is the **Text** property of the **Btn** object.

Methods

A method is an action that an object can perform. For example, the method **Btn.Click()** is the **Click** method of the **Btn** object.

Comments

A comment is an explanatory line in the program code starting with an apostrophe ' character. It's not actually read by the compiler but exists to explain the purpose of the code. For example, **' Clear the list**. might explain a **Clear** statement.

The illustration below shows the Code Editor view of Visual Basic programming code for the Click event-handler of a Button control – line numbering is turned on to aid analysis of the code.

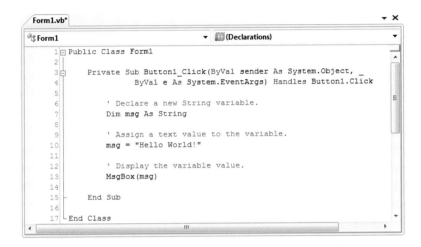

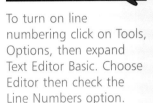
Line-by-line analysis

● Lines 1 and 16 – start and end of the entire Form code

● Lines 3 and 14 – start and end of the Button event-handler

● Lines 5, 8, and 11 – explanatory comments

● Lines 6 – creates a variable called **msg** to store String data

● Lines 9 – places text value into the **msg** variable

● Lines 11 – calls the **MsgBox()** function to show the **msg** value

Syntax high-lighting

● Keywords – Visual Basic core language words appear in blue

● Strings – text values, within double-quotes, appear in red

● Comments – explanatory lines appear in green

● Code – everything else appears in **black**

Declaring variable types

A variable is like a container in a program where a data value can be stored. It is called a variable because its contents can change during the course of the program.

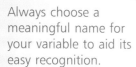
You can create a variable by typing a declaration comprising the Visual Basic **Dim** keyword followed by a unique variable name of your choice. For example, **Dim msg** declares a new variable with the name **msg**.

The variable declaration should also specify the type of data the variable can store using the As keyword followed by one of the Visual Basic data types. So, **Dim msg As String** declares a new variable called **msg** that can store a string of characters.

There are many data types available in Visual Basic programming but those most frequently used are listed in the table below.

Data type	Possible value
Boolean	True or False
String	Characters
Integer	Whole number
Double	Floating-point number

After a variable has been created with a specified data type it can only store data of the type specified in the declaration. For example, you cannot assign a String to an Integer variable.

Data, of the appropriate type, can be assigned to the variable at any point in the program. A variable declaration can also initialize a variable. For example, **Dim msg As String = "Hello"** initializes a new String variable called **msg** with the value **Hello**.

Specifying data types for variables has several advantages:

- It lets you perform specialized tasks for each data type – character manipulation with Strings, validation with Booleans, and arithmetic with Integers and Doubles

- It enables IntelliSense to pop up their features as you type

- It takes advantage of compiler type checking to prevent errors

- It results in faster execution of your code

You can easily display the value stored in any variable by assigning it to the text-based property of visual control, such as a ListBox.

1. Add a ListBox control and a Button control to a Form

2. Double-click on the Button to launch the Code Editor in its event-handler

3. Add these lines to declare and initialize four variables
```
Dim bool As Boolean = False
Dim str As String = "Some text"
Dim int As Integer = 1000
Dim num As Double = 7.5
```

4. Now add these lines to display the stored values
```
ListBox1.Items.Add( "bool value is " & bool )
ListBox1.Items.Add( "str value is " & str )
ListBox1.Items.Add( "int value is " & int )
ListBox1.Items.Add( "num value is " & num )
```

5. Run the application and click the Button to see the value stored in each variable

Hot tip

IntelliSense is the pop-up box that appears as you type in the Code Editor, showing code features.

Beware

Two useful functions are Str(), that converts a number to a string, and Val(), that converts a string to a number. The Str() function was seen in action on page 42 and Val() back on page 31.

Understanding variable scope

The accessibility of a variable is known as its "scope" and depends upon where its declaration is made in the program. A variable's scope determines which parts of the program are able to inspect or change the value stored in that variable.

Variables that are declared within a Sub routine section of code, such as an event-handler, are only accessible within that routine. Reference to them from outside that routine will result in an error as they will not be visible from other routines. A variable declared within a Sub routine is, therefore, said to have "local" scope – it is only accessible locally within that routine.

Local variables are generally declared with the **Dim** keyword, a given name, and a data type specification. The given name must be unique within its own scope but can be used again for another local variable of different scope. For example, two different event-handler Sub routines may both declare a local variable called msg. There is no conflict here as each one is invisible to the other.

Hot tip

Notice that the first line of an event-handler begins with the keywords Private Sub – identifying it as a Sub routine.

60

1 Add three Buttons to a Form

2 Double-click on Button1 to open the Code Editor in its event-handler and add this code
```
Dim msg As String = "Hello from the Button1 Sub"
MsgBox( msg )
```

3 Now double-click on Button2 and add the following code to its event-handler, also declaring a msg variable
```
Dim msg As String = "Hello from the Button2 Sub"
MsgBox( msg )
```

4 Run the application and click these Buttons to confirm the value in each **msg** variable is retrieved without conflict

Beware

Visual Basic projects have a compiler setting called Option Explicit that can enforce proper variable declaration, as described here – always leave this set to On (its default setting) so you will be obliged to declare variables correctly.

VarScope

Hello from the Button1 Sub

OK

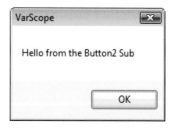

VarScope

Hello from the Button2 Sub

OK

You may often want a variable to be accessible by more than one Sub routine in your program so its declaration will need to be made outside of any Sub routine code. It should, instead, appear in the Form Declarations section, right after the Form Class line at the start of the code. Variables may be declared here with either the **Private** or **Dim** keyword to become accessible throughout the entire Form scope – so any Sub routine can reference them.

The Form Declaration section may also contain variable declarations made with the **Public** keyword to be accessible throughout the entire project, including other Form modules. These are known as "global" variables because they are accessible from absolutely anywhere.

Don't forget

Variable names must be unique within their visible scope.

5 In the Code Editor type these declarations into the Form Declarations section, at the top of the code
Public globalVar As String = "Hello from the Project"
Private formVar As String = "Hello from this Module"

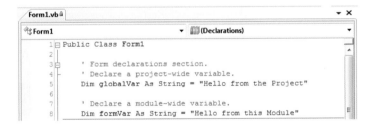

```
Form1.vb
Form1                          (Declarations)
1  Public Class Form1
2
3       ' Form declarations section.
4       ' Declare a project-wide variable.
5       Dim globalVar As String = "Hello from the Project"
6
7       ' Declare a module-wide variable.
8       Dim formVar As String = "Hello from this Module"
```

6 Add this line to the Button3 event-handler subroutine
MsgBox(globalVar & vbCrLf & formVar)

7 Run the application and click on Button3 to retrieve the values from the project-wide and module-wide variables

Hot tip

In deciding where best to declare a variable always make it as local as possible to avoid errors – your first choice should be a local Dim declaration, then a Private module declaration, then a Public global declaration.

Working with variable arrays

The variables introduced so far let you store just one value, but sometimes it's more convenient to deal with a set of values. For example, you might want to store the monthly sales figures for a quarterly period. Rather than create three separate variables named JanSales, FebSales, and MarSales, you can create a single variable array named Sales with three elements – one for each month. You can refer to them as Sales(0), Sales(1), and Sales(2).

1. Add a Button to a Form then create an array variable of 3 elements in its Click event-handler with this code
   Dim Sales(2) As Double

2. Assign values to each element in turn
   Sales(0) = 5245.00
   Sales(1) = 4785.00
   Sales(2) = 7365.50

3. Create a regular variable then assign it the total value of all three array elements
   Dim Quarter As Double
   Quarter = Sales(0) + Sales(1) +Sales(2)

4. Finally, add a statement to display the total value, formatted by the computer's regional currency settings
   MsgBox("Quarter Sales:" & FormatCurrency(Quarter))

5. Run the application to test the result. It is shown here producing the total value formatted in dollars but the formatting depends on the regional settings of the computer on which the application is running.

You may, if you wish, initialize the array elements in its declaration without explicitly specifying the number of elements. The values should be assigned as a comma-separated list within curly braces. In this example the declaration would be
Dim Sales() As Double = { 5245.0, 4785.0, 7365.5 }

Multi-dimensional arrays

Arrays can have more than one dimension. For example, you could create a 2-dimensional array to store the monthly sales of two stores over a quarterly period with **Dim Sales(2,1) As Double**. Individual elements can then be referenced as **Sales(0,0)**, **Sales(1,0)**, **Sales(2,0)**, **Sales(0,1)**, **Sales(1,1)**, and **Sales(2,1)**.

1 Add a Button to a Form then create an array variable of 3x2 elements in its Click event-handler with this code
Dim Sales(2,1) As Double

2 Assign values to each element in turn
Sales(0,0) = 1255 : Sales(1,0) = 1845.5 : Sales(2,0) =1065
Sales(0,1) = 2175 : Sales(1,1) = 2215.5 : Sales(2,1) = 2453

3 Create two regular variables. Assign one the total value of all elements in the array's first dimension and the other the total value of all elements in its second dimension
Dim Store1, Store2 As Double
Store1 = Sales(0,0) + Sales(1,0) +Sales(2,0)
Store2 = Sales(0,1) + Sales(1,1) +Sales(2,1)

4 Finally, add a statement to display the total values, formatted by the computer's regional currency settings
MsgBox("Quarter Sales:" & vbCrLf & _
"Store 1 : " & FormatCurrency(Store1) & vbCrLf & _
"Store 2 : " & FormatCurrency(Store2))

5 Run the application to test the result. It is shown here producing the total values formatted in dollars but the formatting depends on the regional settings of the host computer.

VarArray

Quarter Sales...
Store 1 : $4,165.50
Store 2 : $6,843.50

OK

Performing operations

The Visual Basic arithmetic operators listed in the table below are used to return the result of a calculation.

Operator	Description	Example
+	Addition	16 + 4
-	Subtraction	16 - 4
*	Multiplication	16 * 4
/	Division	16 / 4

In statements using more than one arithmetic operator it is important to specify operator precedence to clarify the expression. For example, the expression **6 * 3 + 5** could return **48 (6 * 8)** or **23 (18 + 5)** – depending which arithmetic is performed first. Adding parentheses around the part to perform first clarifies the expression so that **(6 * 3) + 5** assures the result will be **23** (18 + 5).

The Visual Basic comparison operators listed in the table below are used to test an expression and return a True or False result.

Beware

In Visual Basic the = symbol is used both to assign values and to test for equality – other programming languages have a separate == equality operator.

Operator	Description	Example
=	Equality	num = 10
<>	Inequality	num <> 10
>	Greater than	num > 10
>=	Greater than or equal to	num >= 10
<	Less than	num < 10
<=	Less than or equal to	num <= 10

The Visual Basic arithmetic operators can be used to easily create simple calculation functionality in your application.

1 Add two TextBox controls, four Buttons, and three Labels to a Form and arrange them as below

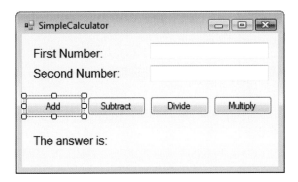

2 Double-click on the Add button to open the Code Editor in its event-handler then type the following statement
Label3.Text = "The answer is : " & _
Str(Val(TextBox1.Text) + Val(TextBox2.Text))

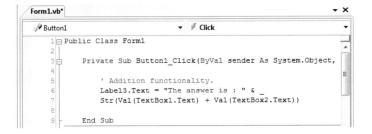

3 Repeat step 2 for the other Button controls but replace the + operator with the appropriate arithmetic operator - for Subtract, / for Divide, and * for Multiply

4 Run the application and enter two numbers, say 16 and 4, into the TextBox fields then click each Button control

Don't forget

Other Visual Basic operators include the ampersand & which is used to concatenate (join) code, and the underscore _ which lets statements continue on the next line.

65

Branching code

Making statements that test an expression allows the program to perform one action or another, according to the result of the test. This important technique is known as "conditional branching" – the code will branch one way or another depending whether a condition is **True** or **False**. In Visual Basic conditional branching can be performed by an **If** statement, using this syntax

```
If ( test-expression-returns-True ) Then
        execute-this-statement
Else
        execute-this-alternative-statement
End If
```

Optionally, multiple expressions can be included in the test using the **And** keyword, where both expressions must be **True**, or the **Or** keyword where either one of the expressions must be **True**.

Don't forget

An If statement must always end with the End If keywords.

1. Add a Label control to a Form

2. Double-click on the Form to open the Code Editor in the Form's Load event-handler

3. Type the following If statement to assign an appropriate value to the Label control according to whether either of the two tested expressions is True
```
If ( WeekDay( Now ) = vbSaturday ) Or _
( WeekDay( Now ) = vbSunday ) Then
        Label1.Text = "Relax – it's the weekend"
Else
        Label1.Text = "Today's a working day"
End If
```

Hot tip

If statements where used back on page 53 to toggle property values, and on page 48, without the optional Else part, to test the status of CheckBoxes and RadioButtons.

4. Run the application – the message will vary depending if the current day is a weekday or a weekend day

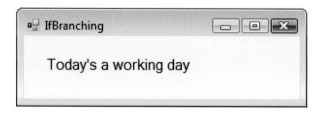

Conditional branching can also be performed with a **Select Case** statement, to provide multiple possible branches, using this syntax

Select Case *expression-to-test*
Case Is *test-returns-True*
            execute-this-statement-then-exit
Case Is *test-returns-True*
            execute-this-statement-then-exit
Case Else
            execute-this-default-statement
End Select

You can add as many **Case** tests as you wish and, optionally, use **Case Else** to provide a final default statement to be executed when none of the tests return **True**.

Hot tip

Try using a Select Case statement to branch code according to the value returned from a MsgBox dialog with Yes, No, and Cancel buttons – as seen on page 36/37.

1. Add a Label control to a Form

2. Double-click on the Form to open the Code Editor in the Form's Load event-handler

3. Type the following Select Case statement to assign an appropriate value to the Label control according to which of the tested Case expressions is True
   ```
   Select Case WeekDay( Now )
   Case Is = vbSaturday
           Label1.text = "It's a Super Saturday"
   Case Is = vbSunday
           Label1.Text = "It's a Lazy Sunday"
   Case Else
           Label1.text = "It's just another working day"
   End Select
   ```

4. Run the application to see an appropriate message

Beware

An If statement must always end with End If keywords and a Select Case statement with the End Select keywords.

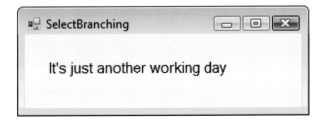

Looping code

Programming loops allow statements within the loop to be executed repeatedly until the loop ends. They must always include a test expression to determine when to end – or they will run forever! The most popular loop in Visual Basic is the **For Next** loop which uses a counter to test the number of times it has executed (iterated) its statements, and has this syntax:

For *counter* = *start* **To** *end*
         execute-this-statement
Next *update-the-counter*

It is often useful to incorporate the increasing value of the counter into the statement/s executed on each iteration of the loop.

 Add a TextBox, Button, and ListBox control to a Form

Double-click on the Button to open the Code Editor in its Click event-handler then type this For Next loop
```
Dim amount As Double = Val( TextBox1.Text )
Dim counter As Integer
For counter = 1 To 10
        ListBox1.Items.Add( "At " & counter & _
        "% interest is " & _
        FormatCurrency( (amount * counter) / 100 ) )
Next counter
```

Run the application, enter a number in the TextBox, then click the Button to run the loop

Beware

The counter variable stores the loop index – do not assign it any other value in the loop.

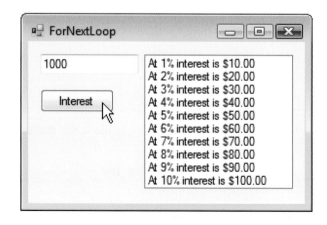

Other types of loop possible in Visual Basic are the **Do Until** loop and the **Do While** loop. Although similar, these two loops are subtly different – a **Do Until** loop executes its statements until the test expression becomes **True**, whereas the **Do While** loop executes its statements until the test expression becomes **False**.

All loops work great to iterate lists of data and are especially useful to iterate the values contained in array elements.

1 Add a ListBox control to a Form

2 Double-click on the Form to open the Code Editor in the its Load event-handler then create this array
**Dim Sales() As Double = { 5601, 8502, 6703, 4204, _
7605, 8206, 9107, 6508, 7209, 5010, 8011, 7012 }**

3 Create a String variable with **Dim sum As String**

4 Now type this Do Until loop then run the application
```
Dim counter As Integer
Do Until counter = Sales.Length
        sum = FormatCurrency( Sales( counter ) )
        counter = counter + 1
        sum = sum & vbTab & MonthName( counter )
        ListBox1.Items.Add( sum )
Loop
```

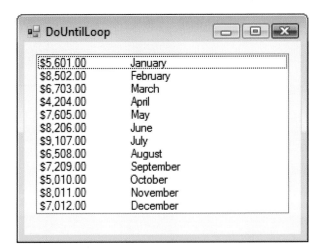

Don't forget

Choose the Do loop which offers greater clarity for your particular purpose – but remember they must both contain a statement to change the counter, and end with the Loop keyword.

Hot tip

The limit of this loop is specified by the Length property of the array. The counter references each element (0-11) from the Sales array and also each month name (1-12) from the Visual Basic MonthName function.

Calling object methods

Visual Basic objects have methods that can be called in code to make the object perform an action at runtime. This works in much the same way that you can write code to assign property values to dynamically change an object's characteristics.

To view any object's available properties and methods type its name followed by a period into the Code Editor. An "IntelliSense" pop-up window will appear showing all that object's properties and methods. Scroll down the list then double-click on an item to add that property or method into the code.

 Add two Label controls and five Buttons to a Form

 In the Properties window set each Label's AutoSize to False, and delete their default Text value

 Make the BackColor of one Label red and name it **RedLbl**, then set the other Label's BackColor to yellow

 Edit the Text property of each Button then arrange the controls so the Form looks like this

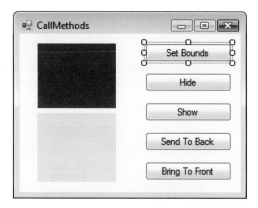

Beware

Leaving the AutoSize property set to the default of True prevents the Label being resized.

 Double-click on the Set Bounds Button to open the Code Editor in its event-handler then type **RedLbl**.

```
RedLbl.
```

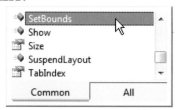

6 Find the **SetBounds** method in the IntelliSense window then double-click it to add it to the code

7 The **SetBounds** method sets the size and position of the control using X, Y, Width, and Height. Add the settings **(45, 45, 45, 100)** to the code, right after the method name

8 Repeat for the other Buttons adding calls to the **Hide()**, **Show()**, **BringToFront()**, and **SendToBack()** methods – no settings are required for any of these

9 Run the application and click each Button to try its action – see the stacking order change from back to front

Don't forget

When you select an item in the IntelliSense window a Tooltip appears containing that item's definition.

Using the With block shorthand

When creating code addressing several properties or methods of an object it can be tedious to repeatedly type the object name.

```
BlueLbl.AutoSize = False
BlueLbl.BackColor = Color.Blue
BlueLbl.Width = 50
Blue.Lbl.Height = 50
BlueLbl.SendtoBack()
```

Usefully, a With block can neatly specify all the values and calls

```
With BlueLbl
        .AutoSize = False
        .BackColor = Color.Blue
        .Width = 50
        .Height = 50
        .SendToBack()
End With
```

Hot tip

Try adding another Label to the Call Methods example then set its properties and methods in the Form's Load event using a With block.

Creating a sub method

When you double-click on a Form or Button to open the Code Editor you see that each event-handler begins and ends like this:

Private Sub ... End Sub

"Sub" is short for "subroutine" and each event-handler subroutine is a Private method of that Form's class. You can create your own subroutine method from scratch that can be called from other code in your application as required.

1   Add Labels, Buttons, and TextBox controls to a Form, then arrange them like this

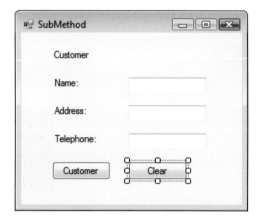

2   Click on View, Code, or press F7, to open the Code Editor then type this code into the Declarations section

```
Private Sub ClearForm()
        TextBox1.Text = ""
        TextBox2.Text = ""
        TextBox3.Text = ""
End Sub
```

3   Click on View, Designer, or press Shift+F7, to return to the Form Designer then double-click on the Clear Button to open the Code Editor in its Click event-handler

4   Type **Me.** and notice that the new ClearForm method has been added to the IntelliSense window. Double-click on it to add **Me.ClearForm()** to the code

5   Run the application, type some text into all three text fields, then click the Button to clear the fields

Sending parameters

A powerful feature of Sub routines is the ability to receive information as they are called. This information is known as "parameters" and is sent from the parentheses of the calling statement to the parentheses of the Sub routine.

In order for a Sub routine to handle parameters it must specify a name and data type for each parameter it is to receive. For example, **str As String** would receive a single string parameter from the caller – it cannot be called unless one string is passed. The Sub routine code can then refer to the passed value using the given name, in this case **str**. Multiple parameters can be passed if the Sub routine specifies the correct number and data types.

1. Click Stop Debugging to return to the Form window shown opposite

2. Now click on View, Code, or press F7, to open the Code Editor then type this code into the Declarations section
```
Private Sub Customer(name As String, addr As String)
        TextBox1.Text = name
        TextBox2.Text = addr
End Sub
```

3. Edit the Customer Button's Click event-handler to include this call to the new Sub routine
```
Me.Customer( "Mike McGrath", "1 Main Street, USA" )
```

4. Run the application and click the Customer Button

73

Creating a function

A Function is similar to a Sub routine, but with one important difference – a Function returns a value to the caller. This means that you must specify the data type of the return value, in addition to specifying parameters, when creating a Function.

1 Add three Labels, a Button, and a TextBox to a Form then arrange them like this

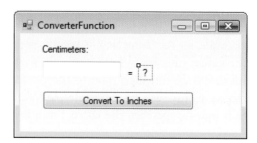

2 Click on View, Code, or press F7, to open the Code Editor then type this code into the Declarations section

```
Private Function Inches(Cm As String) As Double
        Inches = Val( Cm ) / 2.54
        Inches = FormatNumber( Inches , 2 )
        Return Inches
End Function
```

The parentheses specify the parameter Inches must be a String data type – this value is used in the calculation. The result is assigned to the Function name for return as a Double data type, formatted to just two decimal places.

3 Add a call to the Inches Function in the Button's Click event-handler Sub routine

```
Label1.Text = Inches(TextBox1.Text) & " Inches"
```

4 Run the application, enter a number, then click the Button to use the Function

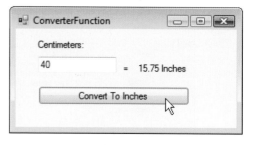

Doing mathematics

The Visual Basic Math object has many methods that are useful when performing mathematical calculations. The most frequently used methods are listed below together with examples returns.

Data type	Description
Math.Ceiling()	Rounds a number up eg: Math.Ceiling(3.5) returns 4
Math.Floor()	Rounds a number down eg: Math.Floor(3.5) returns 3
Math.Round()	Rounds to the nearest integer eg: Math.Round(3.5) returns 4
Math.Sqrt()	Returns the square root eg: Math.Sqrt(16) returns 4
Math.Max()	Returns the larger of two numbers eg: Math.Max(8, 64) returns 64
Math.Min()	Returns the smaller of two numbers eg: Math.Min(8, 64) returns 8
Math.Pow()	Returns a number raised to the specified power. eg: Math.Pow(5, 2) returns 25
Math.Abs()	Returns an absolute value eg: Math.Abs(10.0) returns 10
Math.Cos()	Returns a cosine value eg: Math.Cos(10.0) returns -0.839
Math.Log()	Returns a natural logarithm eg: Math.Log(10.0) returns 2.303
Math.Sin()	Returns a sine value eg: Math.Sin(10.0) returns -0.544
Math.Tan()	Returns a tangent value eg: Math.Tan(10.0) returns 0.648

Hot tip

The Math class also has a Math.PI constant representing the value of π – approximately 3.142.

Don't forget

The returns shown here for Cosine, Log, Sine, and Tangent are rounded to three decimal places – the actual returns provide greater precision.

Generating a random number

Random numbers can be generated by the Visual Basic **Rnd()** function that returns a floating-point value between 0.0 and 1.0. Multiplying the random numbers will specify a wider range. For example, a multiplier of 20 will create a random number between zero and twenty. To make the generated random number more useful you can round it up to the nearest higher integer value with the **Math.Ceiling()** method so the range, in this case, becomes from 1 to 20.

The numbers generated by **Rnd()** are not truly random but are merely a sequence of pseudo random numbers produced by an algorithm from a specific starting point. Whenever an application loads, a call to the **Rnd()** function will begin at the same starting point – so the same sequence will be repeated. This is not generally desirable so the application needs to create a new starting point when it loads to avoid repetition. This can be achieved by calling the **Randomize()** function in the Form's Load event to "seed" the **Rnd()** function with a starting point based upon the system time when the application gets loaded – now the sequence of generated numbers is different each time.

Beware

The numbers generated by the algorithm for Randomize() and Rnd() may be predicted so this technique should not be used for cryptography.

1   Add a Label, TextBox, and Button control to a Form and arrange them like this

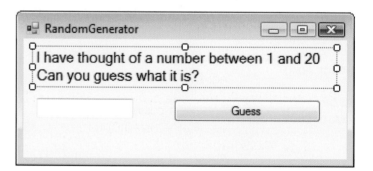

Don't forget

Text in a label will not wrap to the next line unless AutoSize is False.

2   Name the Label control **Msg**, set its AutoSize property to False, then assign its Text property the illustrated text

3   Name the TextBox control **Guess** and set the Text property of the Button likewise

4　Click on View, Code, or press the F7 key, to open the
Code Editor then create a variable in the Declarations

Dim num As Integer

5　Still in the Declarations section add a Sub routine to
assign a random number 1-20 to the **num** variable

Private Sub GetNumber()
       num = Math.Ceiling(Rnd() * 20)
End Sub

6　In the Form's Load event-handler add a call to seed
the random number generator and a call to set the **num**
variable with an initial pseudo random value

Randomize()
GetNumber()

7　Now add some logic to the Button's Click event-handler

Select Case (Val(Guess.Text))
Case Is > num
      Msg.text = Guess.Text & " is too high"
Case Is < num
      Msg.Text = Guess.Text & " is too low"
Case Is = num
      Msg.Text = Guess.Text & " is correct" & _
      "I have thought of another number - Try again!"
      GetNumber()
End Select
Guess.Text = ""

8　Run the application and guess the random number

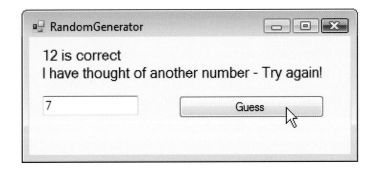

Don't forget

The integer value must
be extracted from the
TextBox by the Val()
function before making
any comparison.

Hot tip

You can use the vbCrLf
constant to format the
contents of the Label.

Summary

- A program's essential elements are Statements, Variables, Functions, Operators, object Properties, and object Methods

- Comment lines help to explain the purpose of the code

- Variable declarations create a variable and can begin with the **Dim**, **Public**, or **Private** keywords

- Each variable declaration should specify the type of data that variable may contain with the **As** keyword and a data type

- **String, Integer, Double**, and **Boolean** are common data types

- Numbers can be extracted from a string by the **Str()** function and a String converted to a number with the **Val()** function

- The **Private** and **Dim** keywords allow local scope – where the variable is only accessible within a procedure or module

- The **Public** keyword allows global scope – where the variable is accessible across an entire program

- A variable array stores values in elements numbered from zero

- Operators are used to perform arithmetic and comparison

- Code can be made to conditionally branch using **If Else** statements or **Select Case** statements

- **For Next** and **Do Until** statements perform code loops

- Object properties and methods can be addressed in code

- A **Function** returns a value but a **Sub** does not

- Values can be sent to a **Sub** routine or a **Function** if they are of the correct data type and of the number specified

- The **Math** object provides many useful methods for performing mathematical calculations

- Pseudo random numbers can be generated by the **Rnd()** function when seeded by the **Randomize()** function

5 Building an application

This chapter brings together elements from previous chapters to build a complete application – from the initial planning stage to its final deployment.

The program plan

When creating a new application it is useful to spend some time planning its design. Clearly define the program's precise purpose, decide what application functionality will be required, then decide what interface components will be needed.

A plan for a simple application to pick numbers for a lottery entry might look like this:

Program purpose

● The program will generate a series of six different random numbers in the range 1 – 49, and have the ability to be reset

Functionality required

● An initial call to start the random number generator

● A routine to generate and display six different random numbers

● A routine to clear the last series from display

Components needed

● Six Label controls to display the series of numbers – one number per Label

● One Button control to generate and display the numbers in the Label controls when this Button is clicked. This Button will not be enabled when numbers are on display

● One Button control to clear the numbers on display in the Label controls when this Button is clicked. This Button will not be enabled when no numbers are on display

● One PictureBox control to display a static image – just to enhance the appearance of the interface

Having established a program plan means you can now create the application basics by adding the components needed to a Form.

1 Open the Visual Basic IDE and create a new Windows Forms Application project called "Lotto"

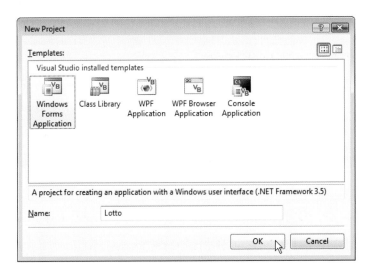

2 In the Form Designer, add six Label controls to the Form from the Toolbox

3 Now add two Buttons and a PictureBox to the Form

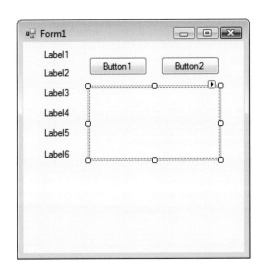

Don't forget

You can drag'n'drop items from the Toolbox or double-click them to add them to the Form.

Assigning static properties

Having created the application basics, on the previous page, you can now assign static values using the Properties window.

1 Click anywhere on the Form to select it then, in the Properties window, set the Form's Text property to "Lotto Number Picker"

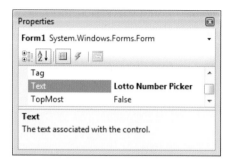

2 Select the Button1 control then, in the Properties window, change its [Name] property to **PickBtn** and its Text property to "Get My Lucky Numbers"

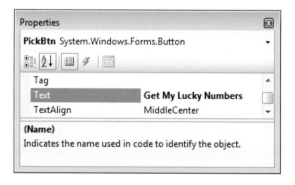

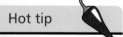
3 Select the Button2 control then, in the Properties window, change its [Name] property to **ResetBtn** and its Text property to "Reset"

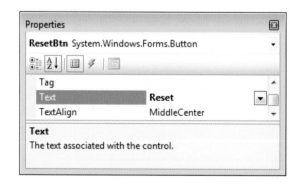

4 Select the PictureBox1 control then, in the Properties window, click the Image property ellipsis button to launch the Select Resources dialog

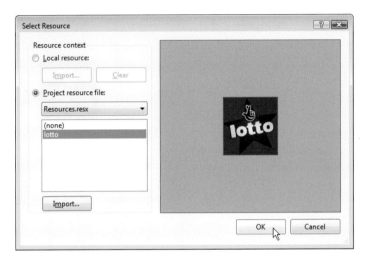

5 Click the Import button, browse to the image location, then click OK to import the image resource – this action automatically assigns it to the PictureBox1 Image property

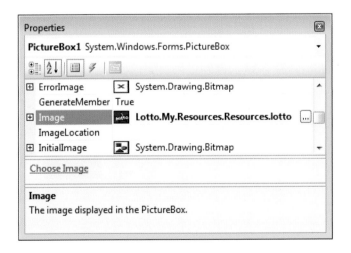

Designing the interface

Having assigned static property values, on the previous page, you can now design the interface layout.

The size of both the PictureBox1 control and the **PickBtn** control first needs to be adjusted to accommodate their content. This can easily be achieved by specifying an AutoSize value so that Visual Basic will automatically fit the control neatly around its content.

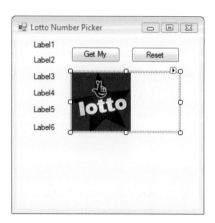

 Select the PictureBox1 control then, in the Properties window, change its SizeMode property to "AutoSize"

 Select the **PickBtn** control then, in the Properties window, set its AutoSize property to "True"

Now you can use the Form Designer's Format menu and Snap Lines to arrange the interface components to your liking.

Hold down the left mouse button and drag around the Labels to select all Label controls

4 Click Format, Align Tops on the Menu Bar to stack the Labels into a pile

5 Click Format, Horizontal Spacing, Make Equal to arrange the pile of Labels into a row

6 Use the Form's right grab handle to extend its width to accommodate the row of Labels and PictureBox1, then drag the row and both Buttons to top right of the Form

7 Drag the PictureBox1 control to top left of the Form, then use the Form's bottom grab handle to adjust its height to match that of the image

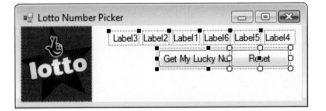

8 Use the Snap Lines that appear when you drag controls around the Form to position the row of Labels and the Buttons to make the interface look like this

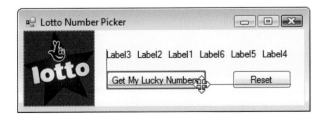

Initializing dynamic properties

Having designed the interface, on the previous page, you can now add some functionality to dynamically set the initial Text properties of the Label controls and the initial Button states.

1 Click View, Code on the Menu Bar, or press F7, to open the Code editor

2 Type the following code into the Declarations section then hit the Return key
Private Sub Clear

The Visual Basic IDE recognizes that you want to create a new subroutine called **Clear**. It automatically adds parameter parentheses after the Sub name and an **End Sub** line to create a subroutine code block.

3 With the cursor inside the new subroutine code block click Edit, IntelliSense, List Members, or press Ctrl+J, to open the IntelliSense pop-up window

4 Scroll down the list of items in the IntelliSense window and double-click on the "Label1" item to add it into the **Clear** subroutine code block

Don't forget

The technique described here demonstrates how to use IntelliSense – but you can, of course, just type the code directly.

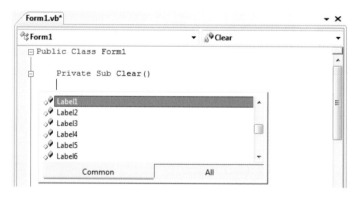

5 Type a period, then double-click the "Text" item when the IntelliSense window reappears to add that code

6 Now type = "..." to complete the line so it reads like this
Label1.Text = "..."

7 Repeat this procedure for the other Label controls – so that the **Clear** subroutine assigns each an ellipsis string

8 With the cursor inside the **Clear** Subroutine code block use IntelliSense in the same way to add these two lines
PickBtn.Enabled = True
ResetBtn.Enabled = False

This completes the **Clear** subroutine functionality by setting the Button states. All that remains is to add a call to the **Clear** subroutine to execute all its instructions when the program starts.

9 In the Form Designer double-click on the Form to open the Code Editor in its Load event-handler and open IntelliSense

10 Scroll down the list in the IntelliSense window and double-click on the "Clear" item you have just created

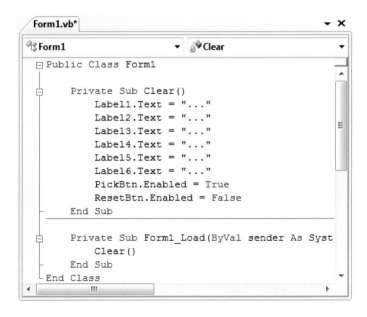

```vb
Form1.vb*

Form1                          Clear
Public Class Form1

    Private Sub Clear()
            Label1.Text = "..."
            Label2.Text = "..."
            Label3.Text = "..."
            Label4.Text = "..."
            Label5.Text = "..."
            Label6.Text = "..."
            PickBtn.Enabled = True
            ResetBtn.Enabled = False
    End Sub

    Private Sub Form1_Load(ByVal sender As Syst
            Clear()
    End Sub
End Class
```

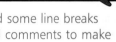

Hot tip

Add some line breaks and comments to make the code more friendly.

Adding runtime functionality

Having created code to initialize dynamic properties, on the previous page, you can now add runtime functionality to respond to clicks on the Buttons.

1   In the Form Designer, double-click on the ResetBtn Button control to open the Code Editor in its Click event-handler then add this call to the Clear subroutine
Clear()

This is all that is needed to provide dynamic functionality for the ResetBtn control. The main dynamic functionality of this application is provided by the PickBtn control which requires the random number generator to be started when the program starts

2   In the Form Designer, double-click on the Form to open the Code Editor in its Load event-handler then add this code to start the random number generator
Randomize()

Now you can create the code to provide dynamic functionality for the PickBtn control itself.

3   In the Form Designer, double-click on the PickBtn Button control to open the Code Editor in its Click event-handler then add this line to declare some variables
Dim i, r, temp, nums(50) As Integer

4   Add a loop to fill the nums array elements 1-49 with the integer values 1 to 49
For i = 1 To 49
        nums(i) = i
Next i

5   Add a second loop to shuffle the values contained in num elements 1-49 – an algorithm to randomize their order
For i = 1 To 49
        r = Int(49 * Rnd()) + 1
        temp = nums(i)
        nums(i) = nums(r)
        nums(r) = temp
Next i

6 Now add the following lines to display the integer values contained in num elements 1-6 in the Label controls
Label1.Text = nums(1)
Label2.Text = nums(2)
Label3.Text = nums(3)
Label4.Text = nums(4)
Label5.Text = nums(5)
Label6.Text = nums(6)

7 Finally, add these two lines to set the Button states ready to reset the application
PickBtn.Enabled = False
ResetBtn.Enabled = True

Beware

The variable declaration creates integer variables called "i", "r", and "temp", along with an integer array called "nums" of 50 elements. Element nums(0) is not actually used though.

Form1.vb*   ▼ ✕

| PickBtn | ▼ | ⚡ Click | ▼ |

```vb
        Private Sub PickBtn_Click(ByVal sender As System

            ' Declare working variables.
            Dim i, r, temp, nums(50) As Integer

            ' Fill elements 1-49 with integers 1 to 49.
            For i = 1 To 49
                nums(i) = i
            Next

            ' Shuffle the values in elements 1-49.
            For i = 1 To 49
                r = Int(49 * Rnd()) + 1
                temp = nums(i)
                nums(i) = nums(r)
                nums(r) = temp
            Next

            ' Display the values in elements 1-6.
            Label1.Text = nums(1)
            Label2.Text = nums(2)
            Label3.Text = nums(3)
            Label4.Text = nums(4)
            Label5.Text = nums(5)
            Label6.Text = nums(6)

            ' Set the Button states to Done.
            PickBtn.Enabled = False
            ResetBtn.Enabled = True
        End Sub
```

Hot tip

Add comments and line breaks like these to clarify the intention of your code when read by someone else – or when you revisit the code later.

Testing the program

Having worked through the program plan, on the previous pages, the components needed and functionality required have now been added to the application – so it's ready to be tested.

 1 Click the Start Debugging button, or press F5, to run the application and examine its initial start-up appearance

The Form's Load event-handler has set the initial dynamic values of each Label control and disabled the reset button as required.

2 Click the **PickBtn** Button control to execute the instructions within its Click event-handler

A series of numbers within the desired range is displayed and the Button states have changed as required – a further series of numbers cannot be generated until the application has been reset.

3 Make a note of the numbers generated in this first series for comparison later

4 Click the **ResetBtn** control to execute the instructions within that Click event-handler and see the application return to its initial start-up appearance as required

5 Click the **PickBtn** Button control again to execute its Click event-handler code a second time

Another series of numbers within the desired range is displayed and are different to those in the first series when compared – good, the numbers are being randomized as required.

6 Click the Stop Debugging button then the Start Debugging button to restart the application and click the **PickBtn** Button control once more

Beware

Failing to call the Randomize() method to seed the Random Number Generator will cause the application to repeat the same sequence each time it runs.

The generated numbers in this first series of numbers are different to those noted in the first series the last time the application ran – great, the random number generator is not repeating the same sequence of number series each time the application runs.

Deploying the application

Having satisfactorily tested the application, on the previous page, you can now create a stand-alone version that can be executed outside the Visual Basic IDE and that can be distributed to others for deployment elsewhere.

Beware

An application cannot be published unless it has been built first.

1 Click Build, Build Lotto on the Menu Bar to build a release version of the application

2 Click Build, Publish Lotto to launch the Publish Wizard

3 Use the wizard's Browse button to select a location where you wish to publish the application – the chosen location shown here is the root directory of removable drive E

Hot tip

When choosing a publish location use the Create New Folder button in the File System dialog to make a folder to contain all the application files.

4 Click the Next button then select whether the user will install the application from a website, network, or portable media such as CD, DVD, or removable drive – in this case accept the default portable media option

5 Click the Next button then select whether the installer should check for application updates – accept the default option not to check for updates in this case

6 Click the Next button to move to the final dialog page, confirm the listed choices, then click the Finish button to publish the application at the specified location

The Publish Wizard generates a number of files including a familiar "setup.exe" executable installer.

7 Move the portable media to the system where it is to be deployed then run **setup.exe** to install the application

When the application is installed on the client system a shortcut is automatically added to the Start Menu which can be used to launch the application. The user can then run the release version of the application just as it performed duing testing of its debug version in the Visual Basic IDE.

The installer also adds an item to the client system's Add/Remove Programs list which can be used to uninstall the application – just like any other Windows program.

Summary

- Always make an initial program plan to avoid the need for time-consuming changes later

- A program plan should clearly define the program purpose, functionality required, and components needed

- Static properties, that will not change when the application is running, can be set at Designtime in the Properties Window

- An AutoSize property value makes Visual Basic automatically fit a control neatly around its content

- The Form Designer's Format menu contains useful features to quickly align and space multiple interface controls

- Snap Lines help you to easily align a selected control to others in the interface at Designtime

- Dynamic properties, that will change when the application is running, can be initialized with the Form's Load event-handler

- The pop-up IntelliSense window lets you easily add program code when using the Code Editor

- Runtime functionality responds to user actions by changing dynamic properties

- A Debug version of an application allows its functionality to be tested as the application is being created in text format

- The Build process compiles a Release version of an application in binary format

- The Publish process creates a final Release version with an installer so the application can be deployed elsewhere

- Applications created with the Visual Basic IDE can be installed and uninstalled just like other Windows applications

6 Solving problems

This chapter describes how to fix errors, debug code, handle exceptions, and get assistance from the Visual Basic Help system.

Real-time error detection

As you type code in the Code Editor window the Visual Basic IDE is constantly monitoring your code for possible errors. When you hit the Return key at the end of each line it examines the line you have just typed and provides realtime feedback of possible errors by adding a wavy underline to questionable code.

Warnings of potential problems are indicated by a green wavy underline. These are not critical and will not prevent execution of the application. A rollover ToolTip explains the warning.

1 In the Code Editor type the following variable declaration in a subroutine block, then hit Return
Dim num As Integer

```
Dim num As Integer
```

2 Place the cursor over the green wavy underline to discover that the warning is merely indicating of a potential problem as the variable has not yet been assigned a value

```
Dim num As Integer
     Unused local variable: 'num'.
```

Errors are indicated by a blue wavy underline. Unlike warnings these are critical and will prevent execution of the application. A rollover ToolTip explains the error.

1 In the Code Editor type the following variable declaration in a Sub routine block, then hit Return
Dim num As Integer =

```
Dim num As Integer =
```

2 Place the cursor over the blue wavy underline to discover that the error is due to a missing value in the expression

```
Dim num As Integer
        Expression expected.
```

Don't forget

Warnings can be ignored but errors must be corrected.

Realtime error detection in the Visual Basic IDE is a fantastic tool to help prevent errors when you are writing code. It not only indicates errors but can even provide a list of correction options.

1. In the Code Editor type the following variable declaration in a Sub routine block, then hit Return
   Dim num As Integr

   ```
   Dim num As Integr
   ```

2. Notice that the blue wavy underline ends with a red box to indicate possible corrections are available. Place the cursor over the blue wavy underline to discover that the error is due to an unknown data type specification

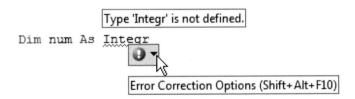

3. Move the cursor over the Smart Tag ! to see an arrow button appear offering error correction options

4. Click the arrow button then choose an option to rectify the error – see your code get corrected accordingly

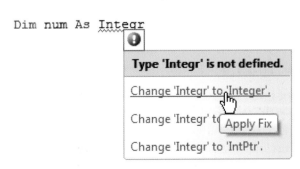

Hot tip

With the cursor over the wavy underline you can press Shift+Alt+F10 to reveal the list of correction options.

Fixing compile errors

While syntax errors like those on the previous page can be detected by the Code Editor in realtime, other errors that employ correct syntax cannot be detected until the code is compiled. Compile errors are typically errors of logic and they cause the execution to halt when an "exception" occurs. For example, when incompatible data types appear in an expression an "InvalidCastException" occurs and execution stops immediately.

1. In the Code Editor type the following lines into a subroutine code block
   Dim num As Double = 7.5
   Dim str As String = "five"
   MsgBox(num * str)

2. Click the Start Debugging button, or press F5, to run the Sub routine and see execution is soon halted. The line causing the exception becomes highlighted in the Code Editor and an Exception Assistant pop-up window appears with a list of possible solutions

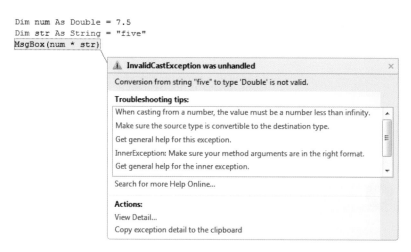

To fix this InvalidCastException the code would obviously need amendment so both expression values are of the Double data type.

The cause of other compile errors may be less obvious without some further investigation. For example, when a loop that is reading array elements attempts to address an element index that does not exist, causing an "IndexOutOfRangeException".

Execution halts immediately so it is useful to examine the counter value to identify the precise iteration causing the compile error.

1 In the Code Editor type the following variable declaration and loop into a Sub routine code block
```
Dim i, nums(10) As Integer
For i = 1 to 20
        nums(i) = i
Next i
```

2 Click the Start Debugging button, or press F5, to run the Sub routine and see execution is soon halted. The code causing the exception becomes highlighted in the Code Editor and an Exception Assistant pop-up window appears with a list of possible solutions

```
Dim i, nums(10) As Integer
For i = 1 To 20
    nums(i) = i
Next i
```

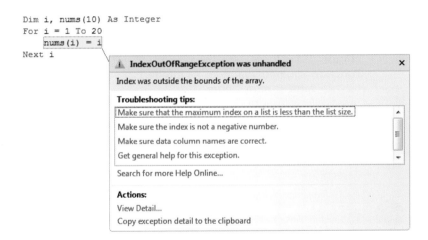

⚠ **IndexOutOfRangeException was unhandled** ✕

Index was outside the bounds of the array.

Troubleshooting tips:

Make sure that the maximum index on a list is less than the list size.

Make sure the index is not a negative number.

Make sure data column names are correct.

Get general help for this exception.

Search for more Help Online...

Actions:

View Detail...

Copy exception detail to the clipboard

3 Place the cursor over the counter variable to see a pop-up appear showing its current value

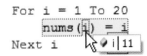
```
For i = 1 To 20
    nums(i) = i
Next i          ● i | 11
```

It's now clear that execution halted when the loop attempted to address nums(11) – beyond the bounds of last element nums(10). To fix this IndexOutOfRangeException the code would need amendment to end the loop after ten iterations.

Beware

Another common compile error is the FileNotFoundException that occurs when a file is missing or its path name is incorrect.

Debugging code

It is sometimes useful to closely examine the progression of a program by watching its execution line by line to locate any bugs. Progress is controlled by clicking the Step Into button on the Menu Bar, or by pressing the F8 key, to move through the entire program one line at a time. When you begin debugging you can also open a Watch window to monitor the value of particular variables as execution proceeds.

1. Double-click on a Form to open the Code Editor in its Load event-handler then add the following code

```
Dim i As Integer
Dim pass As Integer = 0
Dim base As Integer = 2
For i = 1 To 2
        pass = pass + 1
        base = Square( base )
Next i
```

2. Now add the Square function into the Declarations section of the code with these lines

```
Function Square(ByVal num As Integer)
        num = num * num
        Return num
End Function
```

3. Click the Step Into button once, or press F8, to begin debugging

Don't forget

You can click the Stop Debugging button at any time to return to normal Code Editor mode.

4. Click Debug, Windows, Watch on the Menu Bar to launch the Watch window

5. Type the variable name "pass" into the Name column and hit Return, then repeat to add the "base" variable name

Watch			☒
Name	Value	Type	▲
◈ pass	0	Integer	
◈ base	0	Integer	
			▼

6 Click Step Into five times to reach the Square function
call in the first loop iteration and note the variable values

```
For i As Integer = 1 To 2
    pass = pass + 1
    base = Square(base)|
Next
```

Watch			
Name	Value	Type	
pass	1	Integer	
base	2	Integer	

7 Click Step Into eight more times to progress through
each line of the Square function and the loop, returning
to the function call on the second iteration

```
For i As Integer = 1 To 2
    pass = pass + 1
    base = Square(base)
Next
```

Watch			
Name	Value	Type	
pass	2	Integer	
base	4	Integer	

8 Click Step Over once to execute the function without
stepping through each line

```
For i As Integer = 1 To 2
    pass = pass + 1
    base = Square(base)
Next
```

Watch			
Name	Value	Type	
pass	2	Integer	
base	16	Integer	

Hot tip

The Step Out button is used to return to the function caller when you are stepping through lines of a called function.

Setting debug breakpoints

In all but the smallest of programs stepping through each line is very tedious when debugging. Instead, you can quickly reach the part you wish to examine by setting a "breakpoint" to halt execution on a particular line. Setting one or more breakpoints is useful to help you understand how certain Visual Basic code constructs work – such as the nested loop construct shown here.

1️⃣ Double click on a Form to open the Code Editor in its Load event-handler and type this code

```
Dim i, j, k As Integer
Dim pass As Integer = 0
For i = 1 To 3
        For j = 1 To 3
                For k = 1 To 3
                        pass = pass + 1
                Next k
        Next j
Next i
```

2️⃣ In the Code Editor click in the gray margin against each line containing the Next keyword to set three breakpoints – a red dot will appear in the margin and each Next statement is highlighted to indicate the set breakpoints

3️⃣ Click the Start Debugging button, or press F5, and the application will run to the first breakpoint it meets

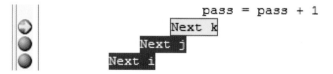

4️⃣ Click Debug, Windows, Locals to launch the Locals window and notice the current value of each variable

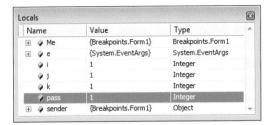

5 Watch the variable values change as you repeatedly click the Start Debugging button to move to each next breakpoint until you reach the third **Next i** statement, then click Step Into to reach the end of the subroutine

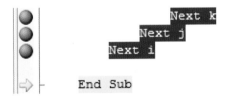

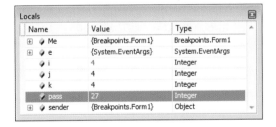

At the end of the subroutine each counter variable has been incremented beyond the upper limit set in the For statements, to exit each loop, and there has been a total of 27 iterations (3x3x3).

6 Click Stop Debugging to finish, then click Start Debugging to once more run to the first breakpoint

7 Click Debug, Windows, Immediate, or press Ctrl+G, to launch the Immediate window

8 In the Immediate window type i = 3 and hit Return, then use the Step Into button to step through each line of the final complete outer loop iteration

Detecting runtime errors

While the Code Editor provides realtime detection of syntax errors, and the compiler provides detection of logic errors, it is the responsibility of the programmer to anticipate user actions that may cause runtime errors when the application is in use. Consideration of all different ways a user could employ your application is important to predict potential runtime errors.

 In a new project add Label, TextBox, and Button controls to a Form so it looks like this

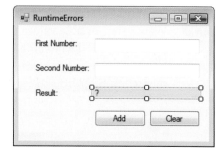

Name the yellow Label "ResultLbl"

Double-click on the Add button to open the Code Editor in its Click event-handler then type the code below to create a simple adding machine

```
Dim num1 As Integer = Val( TextBox1.Text )
Dim num2 As Integer = Val( TextBox2.Text )
ResultLbl.Text = num1 + num2
```

Click Save All, note the location where the project is being saved, then close the Visual Basic IDE

Navigate to the project location and double-click on the executable file in its /bin/Debug folder to run the application outside the Visual Basic IDE

Enter numeric values into each text field then click the Add button to see the application perform as expected

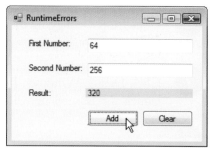

7 Now try adding large numbers like those shown here – an error will occur and the system will produce an error dialog complaining of an overflow

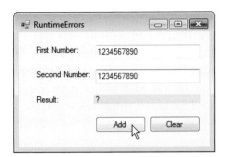

While the programmer may not have intended the application to be used to add such large numbers it is possible the user may wish to do so – and this possibility should have been considered in order to predict this type of runtime error. The overflow has, in fact, occurred because the Integer data type can only store numeric values up to around two billion. This problem can be fixed by changing the variables to use a Long data type instead.

8 Quit the application then edit the Add button's Click event-handler to read like this
```
Dim num1 As Long = Val( TextBox1.Text )
Dim num2 As Long = Val( TextBox2.Text )
ResultLbl.Text = num1 + num2
```

Hot tip

The precise value range of the Integer data type is -2,147,483,648 through 2,147,483,647.

9 Save the amended project then run the application and try to add the two long numbers again

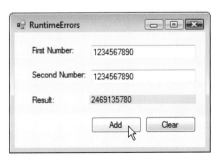

Catching runtime errors

When you are able to predict potential runtime errors by considering all eventualities you can provide code to handle exceptions that may arise with a Try Catch code block. Your program can supply information to the user about the error, should you wish to do so, then proceed normally. This technique could be used to provide code to handle the exception that arose in the previous example instead of the fix suggested.

 Repeat steps 1, 2 and 3 on page 104 to recreate the simple adding machine application then click the Start Debugging button, or press F5, to run the application in Debug mode

Enter two long numbers then click the Add button to attempt the addition – the compiler reports that an OverflowException has occurred

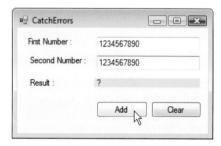

```
Dim num1 As Integer = Val(TextBox1.Text)
Dim num2 As Integer = Val(TextBox2.Text)
ResultLbl.Text = num1 + num2
```

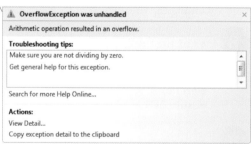

Hot tip

You can use the right-click context menu to quickly switch between the Code Editor and Form Designer.

Click the Stop Debugging button so you can edit the code

Right-click in the Add button's Click event-handler code block then choose Insert Snippet, Common Code Patterns, Exception Handling from the context menu

5 Double-click Try...Catch..End Try Statement to paste a Try Catch code block into the Code Editor

```
Insert Snippet: Code Patterns - If, For Each, Try Catch, Property, etc > Error Handling (Exceptions) >
```

```
                    Define An Exception Class
                    Throw an Exception
                    Try...Catch...End Try Statement
                    Try...Catch...Finally...End Try Statement
                    Try...Finally...End Try Statement
                    Using Statement
```

```
Try

Catch ex As ApplicationException
                 Replace with the specific exception type you want to catch.
End Try
```

Hot tip

Insert Snippet contains lots of useful pieces of code to paste into the Code Editor – take some time to explore its contents.

6 Type OverflowException in place of ApplicationException in the pasted code block

7 Cut'n'paste the original lines of code to put them between the Try and Catch lines

8 Add this code between the Catch and End Try lines MsgBox("Only numbers up to 2 Billion are allowed")

```
Try
    Dim num1 As Integer = Val(TextBox1.Text)
    Dim num2 As Integer = Val(TextBox2.Text)
    ResultLbl.Text = num1 + num2

Catch ex As OverflowException

    MsgBox("Only numbers up to 2 Billion are allowed")

End Try
```

Hot tip

Try adding code to handle the exceptions on page 98 and 99 instead of the suggested fixes.

9 Click Start Debugging then enter long numbers as before and click the Add button to see the exception handled

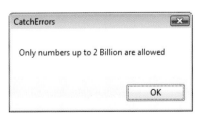

10 Click OK to close the Message Box then change the numbers to be within the range allowed and click the Add button to proceed normally

Getting help

The Visual Basic Help system provides an extensive source of reference to help resolve most problems. For further assistance it also lets you ask questions on MSDN forums. It can be accessed from the Help menu or by pressing the F1 key.

The first time Help is accessed a wizard lets you choose whether to use online sources – this is best unless you don't have a broadband Internet connection. You can edit the sources you prefer to use at any time.

1 Press F1 to start the Help system

2 In the Help window click Tools, Options on the Menu Bar to launch the options dialog

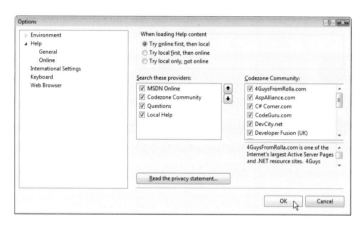

3 Expand the Help menu in the navigation pane then choose the Online item

4 Choose a radio button to determine Online or Local priority

5 Uncheck any Provider or CodeZone Community you do not wish to include, then click OK to save your choices

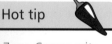

The Help system lets you search the Visual Basic language documentation Index to seek answers to your coding questions. For example, you might need to discover the full range of data types available in Visual Basic programming.

1. Click Help, Index on the Menu Bar, or press Ctrl+Alt+F2, to start the Help system and Index pane

2. Type **data types [Visual Basic]** into the box in the Index pane – the displayed list moves to that entry in the Index as you type

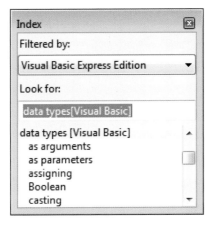

3. Now click on the summary entry that is listed under the data types [Visual Basic] heading to see a table of all data types and possible values appear in the Help window

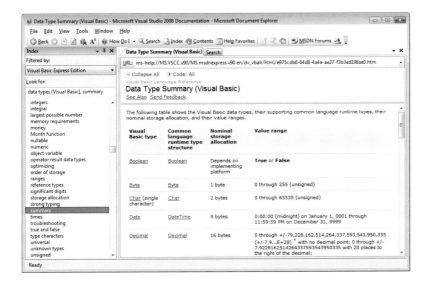

Summary

- The Code Editor constantly monitors your code to provide realtime error detection

- Warnings are not critical and are indicated by a green wavy underline – whereas errors are critical and are indicated by a blue wavy underline

- A red box at the end of a blue wavy underline indicates that a list of possible corrections is available

- Typically, realtime errors are errors of syntax and compile errors are errors of logic

- When a compile error occurs in Debug Mode execution stops and the Exception Assistant offers a list of possible fixes

- In Debug Mode you can discover the current value of any variable simply by placing the cursor over the variable name

- The Step Into button lets you walk through a program one line at a time

- The Step Over button lets you bypass the lines of a called function and the Step Out button lets you return to the line where that function is called

- Variable values can be monitored as a program proceeds using the Watch window or the Locals window

- Breakpoints halt the execution of a program to allow examination of the part of the program where they are set

- In Debug Mode code can be dynamically applied using the Immediate window

- Runtime errors occur when the user action has not been anticipated by the programmer

- Use a Try Catch block to handle anticipated exceptions

- The Help system provides extensive reference sources and online assistance

7 Extending the interface

This chapter demonstrates how applications can incorporate dialogs, menus, multiple forms, and Windows Media Player.

Color, Font & Image dialogs

The Visual Basic IDE makes it simple to add the ability to call upon the standard Windows selection dialogs so the user can choose options within your applications. For example, selection of colors, fonts, and images.

1 Start a new Windows project and add a PictureBox, TextBox, and three Button controls to the Form

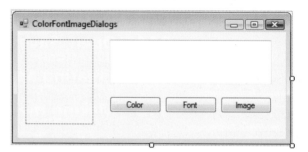

2 Name the Buttons **ColorBtn**, **FontBtn**, and **ImgBtn**

3 From the Dialogs section of the Toolbox add a ColorDialog, FontDialog, and OpenFileDialog component to the Form – see them appear in the Component Tray at the bottom of the Form Designer

 ColorDialog1   FontDialog1    OpenFileDialog1

4 Double-click on the **ColorBtn** Button and add this code to its Click event-handler
```
If ColorDialog1.ShowDialog = _
      Windows.Forms.DialogResult.OK Then
      Me.BackColor = ColorDialog1.Color
End If
```

5 Double-click on the **FontBtn** Button and add this code to its Click event-handler
```
If FontDialog1.ShowDialog = _
      Windows.Forms.DialogResult.OK Then
      TextBox1.Font = FontDialog1.Font
End If
```

6 Double-click on the **ImgBtn** Button and add this code to its Click event-handler

```
If OpenFileDialog1.ShowDialog = _
        Windows.Forms.DialogResult.OK Then
    Try
        PictureBox1.Image = _
        New Bitmap(OpenFileDialog1.FileName)
    Catch ex As ArgumentException
        MsgBox("Not an image")
    End Try
End If
```

Beware

The OpenFileDialog allows the user to select any file. The Try Catch statement handles the ArgumentException that is thrown if the user chooses a file type that is not an image.

7 Click on the Start Debugging button, or press F5, to run the application then click the **ColorBtn** Button to launch the familiar Windows Color selection dialog

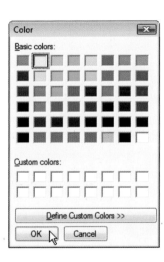

8 Choose a color then click the OK button to apply it to the Form's background

9 Type some text in the TextBox then click the **FontBtn** Button and choose a Font for that text

10 Click the **ImgBtn** Button then browse to select an image to assign to the PictureBox control

Open, Save & Print dialogs

Applications created with Visual Basic can call upon the standard Windows selection dialogs to allow the user to open, save and print files.

1 Start a new Windows project and add a RichTextBox control and three Buttons to the Form – name the Buttons **OpenBtn**, **SaveBtn**, and **PrintBtn**

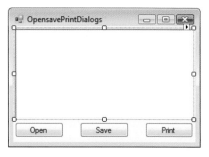

2 From the Dialogs section of the Toolbox add an OpenFileDialog, SaveFileDialog and PrintDialog component to the Form – see them appear in the Component Tray at the bottom of the Form Designer

    OpenFileDialog1   SaveFileDialog1   PrintDialog1

3 Double-click on the **OpenBtn** and add this code to its Click event-handler

```
With OpenFileDialog1
        .Title = "Open File"
        .Filter = "Rich Text Files | *.rtf"
        .FileName = ""
        .CheckFileExists = True
End With

If OpenFileDialog1.ShowDialog = _
        Windows.Forms.DialogResult.OK Then
RichTextBox1.LoadFile(OpenFileDialog1.FileName, _
RichTextBoxStreamType.PlainText)
End If
```

Hot tip

Always define filter options to determine which file types the Open File dialog can see.

4 Double-click on the **PrintBtn** and add this code

```
If PrintDialog1.ShowDialog = _
        Windows.Forms.DialogResult.OK Then
            ' Insert code here to process and print.
End If
```

5 Double-click on the **SaveBtn** and add this code to its Click event-handler

```
With SaveFileDialog1
        .Title = "Save File"
        .Filter = "Rich Text Files | *.rtf"
        .DefaultExt = ".rtf"
        .OverWritePrompt = True
End With

If SaveFileDialog1.ShowDialog = _
        Windows.Forms.DialogResult.OK Then
RichTextBox1.SaveFile(SaveFileDialog1.FileName, _
        RichTextBoxStreamType.RichText)
End If
```

6 Click on the Start Debugging button, or press F5, then use the **OpenBtn** Button to launch the Windows Open File dialog

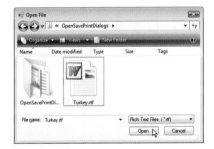

7 Choose a Rich Text Format file then click Open to load it in the RichTextBox control

8 Click the **SaveBtn** Button to launch the Save File dialog and save the loaded file with a different name

9 Click on the PrintBtn Button to launch the familiar Windows Print dialog where you can select Printer preferences before printing

Beware

The Print dialog does not automatically know how to print the document – you need to provide code to enable printing. See page 151 for an example of how to print plain text documents.

115

Creating application menus

Dropdown menus, toolbars, and status bars, like those found in most Windows applications, can easily be added to your own Visual Basic applications from the Toolbox.

1 Find the Menus & Toolbars section of the Toolbox then double-click the MenuStrip item to add it to the Form

2 Click the MenuStrip's arrow button on its Smart Tag then select the option to **Insert Standard Items**

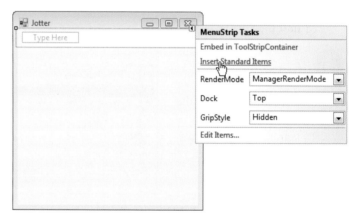

3 When the familiar headings and items have been added to the MenuStrip right-click on any item and use the context menu to edit that item. Also type new custom items into the Type Here boxes as required

Don't forget

You can create your own custom menus using the Type Here boxes instead of Insert Standard Items.

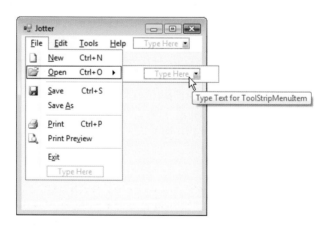

④ In the Toolbox, double-click on the ToolStrip item to add it to the Form then click its Smart Tag button and once more select **Insert Standard Items**

⑤ When the familiar icon buttons have been added to the ToolStrip right-click on any item and use the context menu to edit that item. Also add further custom items from the dropdown list as required

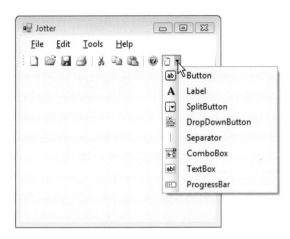

⑥ In the Toolbox, double-click on the StatusStrip item to add it to the Form

⑦ Select the StatusLabel item from the StatusStrip's dropdown list and type "Ready" into the StatusLabel

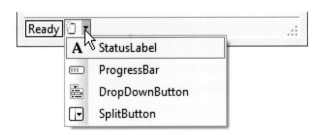

Hot tip

Use StatusBar messages to provide feedback to the user.

⑧ Add a RichTextBox control to the center of the Form, click its Smart Tag button and select the option to **Dock in parent container**, then ensure that its ScrollBars property is set to **Both**

Making menus work

The menu items and toolbar buttons created on the previous page will not perform their desired actions until you add some code to make them work. For actions that feature both in a menu and on a toolbar button it is best to create a Sub routine that can be called from the menu item's Click event-handler and the button's Click event-handler – to avoid duplication.

1 In Form Designer click File, New to select the New menu item

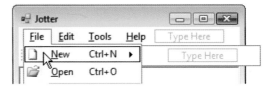

2 Double-click on the New menu item to open the Code Editor in its event-handler and add this call
NewFile()

3 Immediately below the End Sub line of the New menu item's event-handler add this custom Sub routine
Private Sub NewFile()
RichTextBox1.Text = ""
ToolStripStatusLabel1.Text = "Ready"
End Sub

4 Return to the Form Designer then double-click on the New toolbar button to open the Code Editor in that event-handler and add a call to the custom Sub routine
NewFile()

5 Add an OpenFileDialog and SaveFileDialog component from the Dialogs section of the Toolbox

6 In the Click event-handlers of both the Open menu item and the Open toolbar button add this code
OpenFile()

7 Immediately below the End Sub line of the Open menu item's event-handler add this custom Sub routine

```
Private Sub OpenFile()
OpenFileDialog1.Filter = "Text Files | *.txt"
If OpenFileDialog1.ShowDialog = _
        Windows.Forms.DialogResult.OK Then
RichTextBox1.LoadFile(OpenFileDialog1.FileName, _
        RichTextBoxStreamType.PlainText)
End Sub
```

Hot tip

You can add functionality to the File, Exit menu item simply by adding Application.Exit() to its Click event-handler.

8 In the Click event-handlers of both the Save menu item and the Save toolbar button add this code

```
SaveFile()
```

9 Immediately below the End Sub line of the Save menu item's event-handler add this custom Sub routine

```
Private Sub SaveFile()
SaveFileDialog1.Filter = "Text Files | *.txt"
If SaveFileDialog1.ShowDialog = _
        Windows.Forms.DialogResult.OK Then
RichTextBox1.SaveFile(SaveFileDialog1.FileName, _
        RichTextBoxStreamType.PlainText)
End Sub
```

119

10 Run the application and test the functionality of the New, Open, and Save file menu items and toolbar buttons

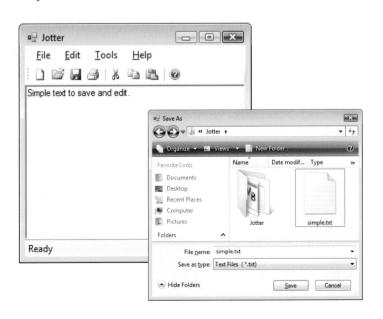

Don't forget

Keyboard shortcuts are already configured – try Ctrl+N, Ctrl+S, and Ctrl+O to test them.

Adding more forms

Most Windows applications have more than one Form – even the simplest application usually has an About dialog, and perhaps a Splash Screen, to provide version information to the user. These can easily be added to your applications in Visual Basic.

1 Click Project, Add New Item on the Menu Bar, to launch the Add New Item dialog, then select the About Box icon and click the Add button – see a new Form file called **AboutBox1.vb** get added in the Solution Explorer

2 In Solution Explorer right-click on the top project icon then select Properties from the context menu, or click Project, Properties on the Menu Bar, to open the Project Designer window

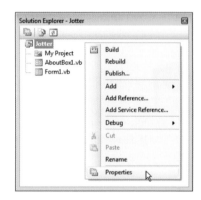

3 In the Project Designer click the Assembly Information button and modify the Copyright, Description, and Company fields to your preference, then click the OK button

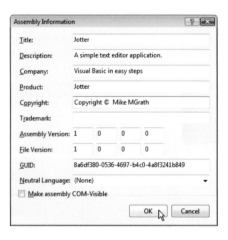

4 In Form Designer double-click on the About item in the Help menu then add this code to its Click event-handler
AboutBox1.ShowDialog()

5 Click Start Debugging, or press F5, to run the application then click Help, About to see the About dialog

6 In Form Designer double-click on the "Hide Form 2" Button in Form 2 and add this code to its Click event-handler
Me.Hide()
Form1.Show()

7 Now double-click on the "Close Form 2" Button in Form 2 and add this code to that Click event-handler
Me.Close()
Form1.Show()

8 Click Start Debugging, or press F5, to run the application and click the "Hide Form 1" Button – Form 1 disappears and Form 2 appears

9 Type something into the TextBox then click on the "Hide Form 2" Button – Form 2 disappears, and Form 1 reappears

10 Click the "Show Hidden Value" Button in Form 1 – the text you typed into the TextBox in Form 2 gets copied into the **ValueLbl** Label in Form 1

11 Click "Hide Form 1" once more then type something else in the TextBox and click the "Close Form 2" button

12 Click the "Show Hidden Value" Button in Form 1 again – nothing is displayed in the **ValueLbl** Label as your input has been lost

Hot tip

Try creating a variable to store the value in the TextBox when Form 2 gets closed so the user input can be recalled.

Playing sounds

Sound files can be included within an application as a resource, in much the same way that image files can be imported as a resource, to enhance the application. These can then be played, as required, by calling upon the Windows Media Player on the local system.

1 Start a new Windows Application project and add a single Button control to the Form

2 In Solution Explorer, right-click on the top project icon then choose Properties from the context menu to open the Project Designer window

3 In Project Designer select the Resources side tab, then the Audio item from the Strings dropdown list

4 Select the Add Existing File... item from the Add Resource dropdown list to launch the Add File dialog

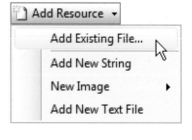

Don't forget

You can add an icon resource and assign it to the Form's Icon property in its Load event-handler.

5 Browse to the location of the sound file you wish to add then click the Add button – see the sound file **tada.wav** get added to the Resources folder in Solution Explorer

6 Click the X button to close the Project Designer and click Yes when asked if you want to save changes

7 Click View, Code, or press F7, to open the Code Editor then add this line to the Declarations section
Friend WithEvents player _
          As New System.Media.SoundPlayer

8 In Form Designer double-click on the Button then add the following code to its Click event-handler
player.Stream = My.Resources.tada
player.Play()

9 Click Start Debugging, or press F5, to run the application, then click the Button to play the sound

Playing multimedia

A Visual Basic application can employ an ActiveX instance of the Windows Media Player to play all types of local media files within the application interface.

1 Start a new Windows Application and add a Button control to the Form and an OpenFileDialog component

2 In the Toolbox right-click on the Components section and select Choose Items from the context menu

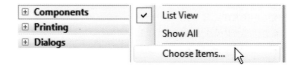

3 When the Choose Toolbox Items dialog appears click its **COM Components** tab, then check **Windows Media Player** and click OK – a new Windows Media Player item gets added to the Toolbox' Components section

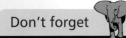
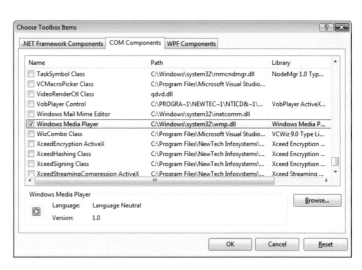

4 From the Toolbox, add a Windows Media Player component to the Form and resize it so its display and controls are fully visible – note that component is called **AxWindowsMediaPlayer1**

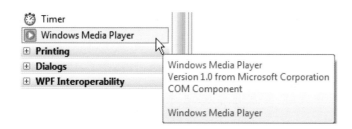

5 In Form Designer, double-click on the Button to open
the Code Editor in its Click event-handler and add the
following code

```
With OpenFileDialog1
  .Title = "Media File Browser"
  .Filter = "Media Files (*.wmv;*.mp3)|*.wmv;*.mp3"
  .FileName = ""
  .CheckFileExists = True
End With

If OpenFileDialog1.ShowDialog = _
       Windows.Forms.DialogReult.OK Then
AxWindowsMediaPlayer1.URL = _
       OpenFileDialog1.Filename
End If
```

6 Run the application then click the Button control to
launch the OpenFileDialog and choose a valid media file
– see it start playing in the application interface

Beware

Notice how multiple
file formats must be
separated by a
semi-colon in the Filter
statement.

Hot tip

Try adding a Status bar
to display the name of
the file currently playing.

Summary

- The Dialogs section of the Toolbox contains components that can be added to an application to call upon the standard

- Windows dialogs to select Colors, Fonts, Images, and Files

- Open File and Save File dialogs can be configured to filter file types so they only display files of a specified file extension

- A Print dialog allows the user to select printer options but it cannot automatically print

- Familiar menus can easily be added to an application using the Insert Standard Items option of the MenuStrip component

- The ToolStrip component provides familiar toolbar icons

- You can add a StatusStrip component to provide an application status bar to display feedback to the user

- Where both MenuStrip and ToolStrip components appear in an application it is best to create Sub routines to be called when the user chooses a menu item or associated icon

- A MenuStrip component automatically provides keyboard shortcuts for each of its menu items

- The Add New Item option on the Project menu can be used to add a Form, About Box dialog, and Splash Screen

- Multiple forms can be controlled using their **Show()**, **Hide()**, and **Close()** methods

- Applications can be enhanced by including audio files in their Resources folder to provide sound

- Windows COM components can be added to the standard selection of components on the Visul Basic Toolbox

- An ActiveX instance of Windows Media Player can be added to an interface to allow the application to play multimedia files

8 Scripting with Visual Basic

This chapter illustrates how Visual Basic may be used outside the Visual Basic IDE to add functionality to Microsoft Office applications and to add interactive features to web pages.

An introduction to VBA macros

Visual Basic for Applications (VBA) is the programming language built into Microsoft Office applications. It shares the same core Visual Basic language as that in the Visual Basic IDE but has different available objects in each application – Word has an ActiveDocument object and Excel has an ActiveSheet object.

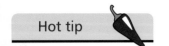
Where Microsoft Office is installed on a system all Office objects are available across all versions of Visual Basic. So you can program Word from Excel, or from a standalone application created in the Visual Basic IDE.

VBA has a Form Designer and Debugger much like those in the Visual Basic IDE but with a more limited set of features.

Run Button   Properties Window   Project Window

Form Designer

Toolbox

Code Editor

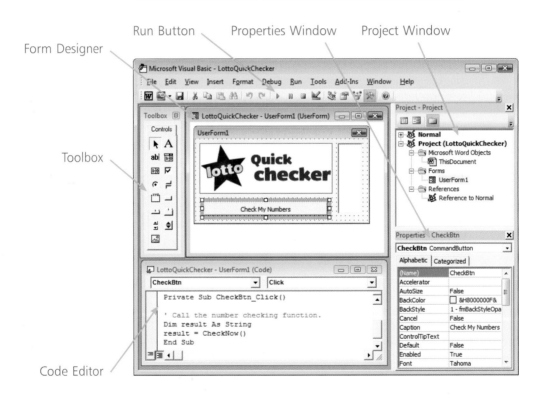

You cannot create standalone executable applications with Visual Basic for Applications, as it has no native code compiler, but you can create a script, hidden within the document file, to execute a series of instructions upon the document. This is known as a "macro" and is typically used to automate a task you perform regularly that requires multiple commands. For example, to insert a table with a specific style and number of rows and columns.

1 Launch Microsoft Word, or any other Office 2007 application, then click the Developer tab and choose the Visual Basic ribbon icon to launch the Visual Basic Editor

2 In the Visual Basic Editor, click Insert, Module to open the Code Editor window

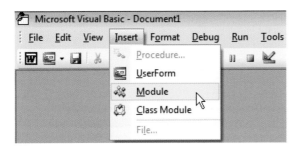

131

3 In the Code Editor, type this Visual Basic subroutine
Private Sub Hello()
  MsgBox("Hello from VBA!")
End Sub

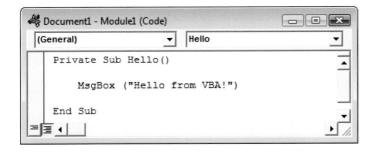

4 In the Visual Basic Editor, click the Run button or press F5 to execute the subroutine – the Visual Basic Editor gets minimalized until you click the OK button in the Message Box

Creating a Word macro

Bookmarks can be inserted into a Word document to indicate the position at which a macro should insert content.

1. Open a new document in Word, type some text, then use Insert, Bookmark to add a bookmark – name it "mark"

2. Click Developer, Visual Basic, or press Alt+F11, to launch the Visual Basic Editor

3. In the Visual Basic Editor, click Insert, Module to open the Code Editor window

4. Now type the following code into the Code Editor

```
Sub AddTable()
   If ActiveDocument.Bookmarks.Exists("mark") Then
   ActiveDocument.Bookmarks("mark").Select
   Set tbl = ActiveDocument.Tables.Add(Range:= _
      Selection.Range, NumRows:=3, NumColumns:=9)
   tbl.AutoFormat Format:=wdTableFormatClassic2
   End If
End Sub
```

5. Click the Run button, or press F5, to run the macro – see a formatted table appear at the bookmark position

Hot tip

You can use the Edit, Undo menu in Word to reverse the two steps performed by VBA to Add and Format this table.

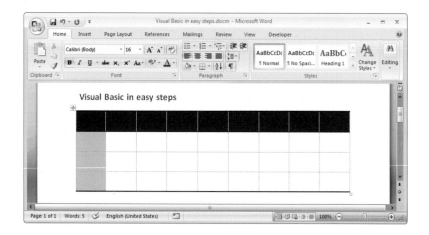

When you have created a macro that you wish to make available for use in other documents the macro can be stored inside Word's master template **Normal.dotm** and added as a Word menu item.

1 Select Developer, Macros to open the Macros dialog, then click the Organizer button

2 Choose the Macro Project Items tab, select the macro module from the current document list, then click the Copy button to copy the macro to **Normal.dotm**

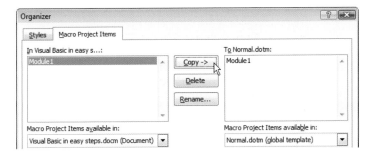

3 Close the Organizer and the current document then start a new document and insert a bookmark named "mark"

4 Click the Word toolbar and choose "Customize Quick Access Toolbar" to launch the Options dialog

5 In the Options, Customize dialog, select to Choose Commands from Macros, then add the **AddTable** module and click OK to add an icon to the Quick Access Toolbar

6 Click the newly added **AddTable** macro icon on the Quick Access Toolbar to run the macro – once more adding a formatted table at the bookmark position

Hot tip

The Run button on the Macros dialog can be used to run any macro stored in Normal.dotm – without creating a custom menu item.

Creating an Excel macro

Values can be inserted into cells of an Excel spreadsheet by a macro that uses a loop to move through a range of cells.

1 Open a worksheet in Excel then click Developer, Visual Basic, or press Alt+F11, to launch the Visual Basic Editor

2 In the the Visual Basic Editor, click Insert, Module to open the Code Editor window

3 Now type the following code into the Code Editor

```
Private Sub AddMonthNames()
Dim i As Integer
i = 0
Do Until i = 12
        Set currentCell = ActiveSheet.Cells( _
          ActiveCell.Row + i , ActiveCell.Column)
        i = i + 1
        currentCell.Font.Bold = True
        currentCell.Font.Color = vbRed
        currentCell.Value = MonthName( i )
Loop
End Sub
```

4 Select any cell in the worksheet then click the Run button, or press F5, to run the macro – see bold red month names appear in cells down the current column, starting at the selected cell

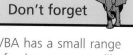

Don't forget

VBA has a small range of color constants, like the vbRed constant seen here. Refer to VBA Help to discover a full list.

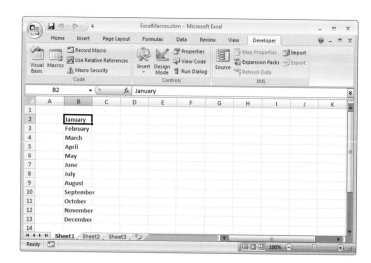

Excel macros can be run automatically when a Worksheet gets loaded, or manually using a keyboard shortcut or Button control.

1 In the Project Window, right-click on the **ThisWorkbook** icon and choose View Code from the context menu

2 From the dropdown list at the top of the Code Editor select the Workbook item then add this code
Private Sub Workbook_Open()
MsgBox("Workbook opened at "+ Str(Time))
End Sub

3 Close the Visual Basic Editor then click Macros, Options and add a shortcut key letter of your choice to the **Ctrl+** statement in the Options dialog

4 On the Developer tab click Insert, ActiveX button control then click an empty cell to place a Button control there

5 Double-click the Button control to open the Code Editor in its Click event-handler then add this Call statement
Call AddMonthNames()

6 Save the changes and close the worksheet – reopen the worksheet to see the MessageBox appear then use the Button, or your keyboard shortcut, to run the macro

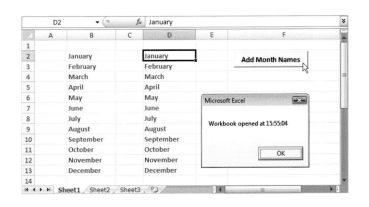

Hot tip

Use the Design Mode button on the Developer tab when you want to edit or move controls on a worksheet.

Running advanced macros

More advanced macros can be created to control one Office application from within another. Typically you may want to include information from an Excel spreadsheet within a Word document using a macro to get the information automatically.

1 Open Excel and add some data in cell B2. Name this cell "Total", then save the Workbook as "Sales.xlsx" in your Documents folder and close Excel

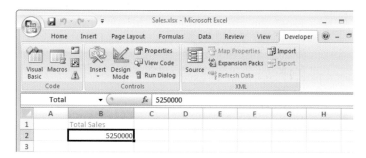

2 Start a new Word document then insert a Bookmark and also name it "Total" – it doesn't need to have the same name as the Excel cell but it is convenient

3 Open the Visual Basic Editor then click Tools, References to launch the References dialog – check the reference for the Microsoft Excel Object Library then click OK

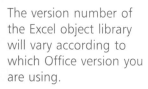
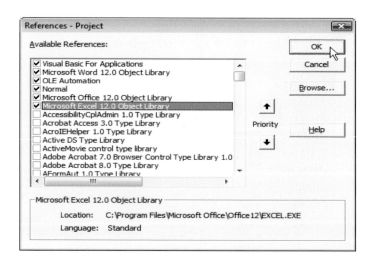

4 In the the Visual Basic Editor, click Insert, Module to open the Code Editor window

5 Now type the following code into the Code Editor, modifying the path to suit the location of your "Sales.xlsx"

```
Private Sub GetTotal()
Set xl = CreateObject("Excel.Application")
xl.Workbooks.Open ("C:\Users\Mike\Documents\Sales.xlsx")
xl.Worksheets("Sheet1").Activate
ActiveDocument.Bookmarks("Total").Select

Dim sum As String
sum = FormatCurrency( _
        xl.ActiveSheet.Range("Total").Value, 0)
Selection.InsertAfter (sum)

xl.Workbooks.Close
Set xl = Nothing
End Sub
```

6 Click the Run button, or press F5, to run the macro and see the value retrieved from the Excel cell get formatted into the local currency and appear in the Word document

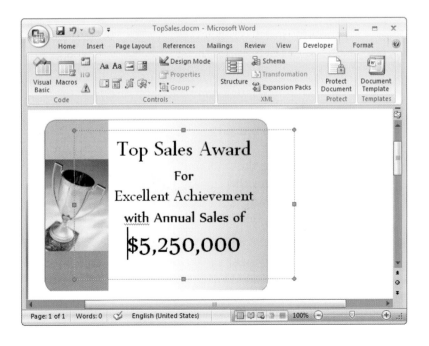

Beware

Remember to have the macro close the Workbook and release Excel after it has retrieved the cell value.

An introduction to VBScript

VBScript is a scripting language that, like VBA, shares the same core Visual Basic language as that found in a Visual Basic IDE. Scripts written in VBScript are interpreted by a script "engine" that processes the instructions to execute the script. The script engine can be invoked either from within the Windows GUI, or at a Windows Command Prompt, or by Internet Explorer.

Unlike the Visual Basic IDE, and VBA, there is no development environment for VBScript – you simply create your scripts in any plain text editor.

1 Open a plain text editor, such as Windows Notepad, then type the following code
MsgBox "Hello from VBScript!", vbExclamation

2 Name this file "Hello.vbs" and save it on your Desktop

3 Double-click on the file icon to invoke the script engine from the Windows GUI to execute the script – see the Message Box appear

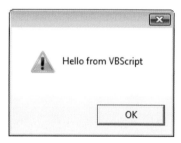

4 Launch a Command Prompt window, then use the CD command to navigate to your Desktop directory

5 Now type the command **Hello.vbs** and hit Return to invoke the script engine from the Command Prompt – see the Message Box appear again

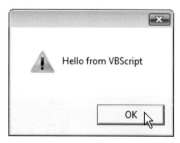

6 Open Notepad, or your favorite HTML editor, then type the web page source code shown below

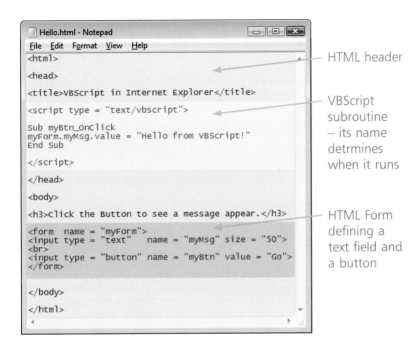

— HTML header

— VBScript subroutine – its name detrmines when it runs

— HTML Form defining a text field and a button

7 Save the file as "Hello.html" then open it in Internet Explorer and click the button to run the script

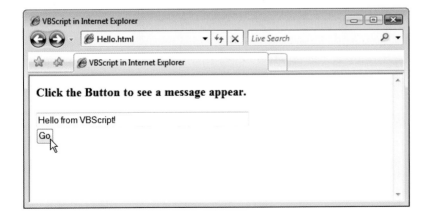

Scripting for Internet Explorer

In order to make scripts respond to events within Internet Explorer each subroutine must be carefully named using the object name and event name, separated by an underscore character. Clicking an HTML button fires its **onClick** event – so a subroutine to respond when a button called "myBtn" is clicked would have to be be named **myBtn_onClick**.

Common events are listed in the table below with brief descriptions and example subroutine names.

Event	Description	Example Sub Name
onClick	Object is clicked	**myBtn_onClick**
onChange	Text is changed	**myTxt_onChange**
onFocus	Object gets focus	**myTxt_onFocus**
onBlur	Object loses focus	**myTxt_onBlur**
onSelect	Text is selected	**myTxt_onSelect**
onMouseOver	Mouse hovers	**myObj_onMouseOver**
onSubmit	Form is submitted	**myForm_onSubmit**

Objects available to VBScript in Internet Explorer are arranged hierarchically, following its Document Object Model (DOM). Uppermost is the **Window** object that has properties and methods concerning the current browser window. For example, you can call the **Window.Open()** method to launch a new pop-up window.

The **Document** object on the first tier level of the DOM hierarchy has properties and methods about the current document page. For example, the **Window.Document.Title** property contains the page title, as stated between the HTML **<title>** tags.

Optionally, you may omit the uppermost part when addressing any first-tier object, so the **Window.Document.Write()** method, for example, can be addressed simply as **Document.Write()**.

Lower-level objects can be addressed using the DOM hierarchy or by the value assigned to their HTML **name** attributes. For example, if the first HTML form in a document is named "myForm", and the first element in that form is named "myMsg", the value in that element can be addressed as **myForm.myMsg.Value** or as **Window.Document.Forms(0).Elements(0).Value**.

1   Make a copy of the **Hello.html** file, listed on page 139, and save it as **Dom.html**

2   Delete all the previous VBScript code in the script block – everything between the **<script>** and **</script>** tags

3   In the script block type the following new subroutine to address objects using the DOM hierarchy

```
Sub Window_onLoad
Window.Document.BgColor = vbGreen
Window.Document.Forms(0).Elements(0).Value = _
"Welcome to " & Window.Navigator.AppName
End Sub
```

4   In the script block type the following new subroutine to address objects by their HTML **name** attribute values

```
Sub myBtn_onClick
MsgBox myForm.myMsg.Value
End Sub
```

141

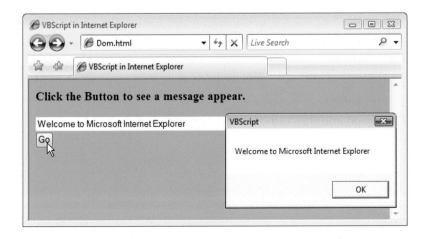

Scripting ActiveX objects

Internet Explorer is able to include ActiveX controls within an HTML document and VBScript can be used to address their properties and methods. ActiveX controls used in this way do perform well, because they run as native code on the user's system, but only if the user has first installed and registered those controls. It is, therefore, best to only use ActiveX controls in HTML documents on an Intranet – where you can be sure users will already have the required ActiveX controls.

Each ActiveX control has a unique identification number. This is hidden from you in the Visual Basic IDE but must appear in the source code of an HTML document so Internet Explorer can recognize the ActiveX control. The number must first be assigned to the **classid** attribute of an HTML **<object>** tag then VBScript can address its properties and methods, as with any other object.

1   Copy the following code between the body and tags of a new HTML document, to add two ActiveX controls – a Calendar and a Microsoft Agent

```
<object id = "Calendar1" classid =
    "CLSID:8E27C92B-1264-101C-8A2F-040224009C02">
</object>

<object id = "AgentControl" classid =
    "CLSID:D45FD31B-5C6E-11D1-9EC1-00C04FD7081F">
</object>
```

2   Add this variable declaration and subroutine to the HTML document's script block, between the script tags, to initialize the Microsoft Agent control when Internet Explorer loads the document

```
Dim Merlin

Sub Window_onLoad
AgentControl.Characters.Load("Merlin")
Set Merlin = AgentControl.Characters("Merlin")
Merlin.Show
Merlin.Speak("Click the ActiveX calendar to choose a day")
End Sub
```

3   Save the document then open it in Internet Explorer

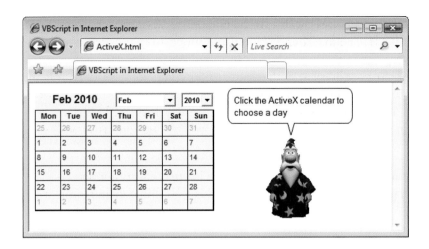

Providing the user has the appropriate ActiveX controls Internet Explorer will display them, and the character "speaks" the text.

4 Now add this subroutine to the script block, to handle the Calendar control's Click event, then reload the page and click any day on the Calendar control

```
Sub Calendar1_Click
Merlin.Speak("Thank you for choosing " & _
        MonthName(Calendar1.Month) & _
        ", " & Calendar1.Day)
End Sub
```

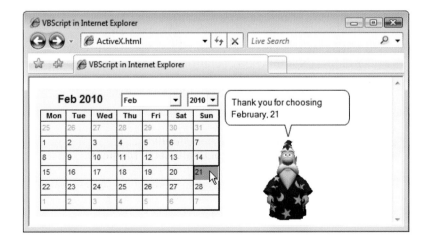

143

Running dynamic web scripts

Dynamic HTML (DHTML) effects can be achieved using VBScript in Internet Explorer to respond to user actions on the page. This simply requires event-handlers to change some aspect of the page to provide feedback to the user.

The most common DHTML effect uses the **onMouseOver** event to change the appearance of an item on the page when the user places the mouse cursor over that item. Similarly, the **onMouseOut** event can revert the item to its original appearance when the user moves the cursor off the item. This is often called a "rollover" effect from its resemblance to a pinball machine action.

Taking this effect further, additional changes can be applied in response to the **onMouseDown** and **onMouseUp** events that occur when the user clicks and releases the mouse button when on the item – so the item can have four possible dynamic states.

Individual elements of an HTML document can usefully be addressed simply by the unique value assigned to their **id** attribute and their appearance modified by changing their styles to provide rollover effect feedback to the user.

Beware

Be sure to copy the style sheet rules accurately – omitting a colon or semi-colon may not apply all the styles correctly.

1 Type the following code into the body section of a new HTML document to create an item for the rollover effect
```
<div id = "r1">OUT</div>
```

2 Copy the following style sheet into the head section of the document to define the item's initial appearance
```
<style type = "text/css">
#r1     { width:150px; height:30px; text-align:center;
          font-size:20pt; padding:10px; color: red;
          background:silver; border:8px outset red }
</style>
```

3 Add this subroutine to the HTML document's script block to handle the item's **onMouseOver** event
```
Sub r1_onMouseOver
r1.innerHTML = "OVER"
r1.style.color = "green"
r1.style.background = "lime"
r1.style.border = "8px outset green"
End Sub
```

4 Add this subroutine to the HTML document's script block to handle the item's **onMouseOut** event

Sub r1_onMouseOut
r1.innerHTML = "OUT"
r1.style.color = "red"
r1.style.background = "silver"
r1.style.border = "8px outset red"
End Sub

Hot tip

Routines that await events are sometimes referred to as "listeners".

5 Add this subroutine to the HTML document's script block to handle the item's **onMouseDown** event

Sub r1_onMouseDown
r1.innerHTML = "Down"
r1.style.color = "olive"
r1.style.background = "yellow"
r1.style.border = "8px inset olive"
End Sub

6 Add this subroutine to the HTML document's script block to handle the item's **onMouseUp** event

Sub r1_onMouseUp
r1.innerHTML = "Up"
r1.style.color = "blue"
r1.style.background = "aqua"
r1.style.border = "8px outset blue"
End Sub

7 Save the file then run it in Internet Explorer and test the rollover as your mouse creates four dynamic states

Don't forget

You can also create image rollovers, that swap the image assigned to the src attribute of an <img> tag. Other popular dynamic effects change the location, or visibility of items.

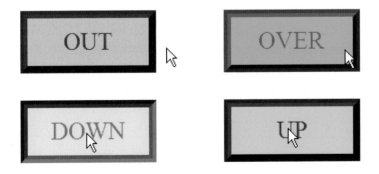

Summary

- Visual Basic for Applications (VBA) is built into all Microsoft Office applications, but each application has unique objects

- The VBA environment is similar to that of the Visual Basic IDE but it can't produce standalone executable applications

- A macro can insert content into a Word document at the position indicated by an inserted bookmark

- Saving macros in the **Normal.dotm** master template makes them available for use in other Word documents

- Loops can be used in a VBA macro to read or write a range of cells within an Excel spreadsheet

- Advanced macros allow one Office application to be controlled from within another one

- There is no development environment for VBScript – scripts are created in any plain text editor such as Windows Notepad

- The script engine that interprets VBScript instructions can be invoked from within the Windows GUI, at the Command Prompt, or by Internet Explorer

- VBScript subroutines for Internet Explorer must be named using the object name and event name, separated by an underscore, so the browser can recognize the event handler

- Internet Explorer's Document Object Model (DOM) arranges its objects hierarchically, with the Window object at the top

- Lower-level objects can be addressed either by their full DOM address, **name** attribute value, or **id** value

- ActiveX controls can be included in an HTML document if that control is available on the user's system

- VBScript can create Dynamic HTML (DHTML) effects by changing the appearance of items in response to user actions

9 Harnessing data

This chapter shows how Visual Basic applications can import data from a variety of external sources.

Reading text files

The **My.Computer.FileSystem** object has methods that make it easy for Visual Basic applications to work with local files. Text can be imported using its **ReadAllText()** and exported using its **WriteAllText()** method to append text to an existing file, or create a new file. Files can be removed with the **DeleteFile()** method or their existence confirmed with the **FileExists()** method.

1 Start a new Windows Forms Application then add two TextBox controls and three Button controls to the Form

2 Set the Multiline property of Textbox2 to True then name the buttons **WriteBtn, ReadBtn**, and **DeleteBtn**

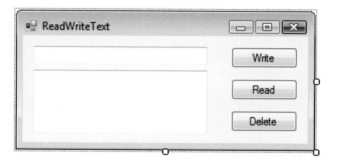

3 Press F7 to open the Code Editor then create a path variable in the Declarations section, modifying the path to suit the Documents directory location on your system
Dim myFile As String = "C:\Users\Mike\Documents\log.txt"

Don't forget

Remember to include the third True parameter to append text to a file.

4 Double-click on the **WriteBtn** to open the Code Editor and add the following code to its Click event-handler
```
My.Computer.FileSystem.WriteAllText( _
        myFile, TextBox1.Text & vbCrLf, True)
TextBox1.Text = ""
```

5 Return to the Form Designer then double-click the **ReadBtn** and add this code to its Click event-handler
```
Try
TextBox2.Text = _
My.Computer.FileSystem.ReadAllText( myFile )
Catch ex As Exception
TextBox2.Text = "Unable to read from  " & myFile
End Try
```

6 Return to the Form Designer then double-click the
DeleteBtn and add this code to its Click event-handler

```
TextBox1.Text = ""
TextBox2.Text = ""
If My.Computer.FileSystem.FileExists( myFile ) Then
My.Computer.FileSystem.DeleteFile( myFile )
End If
```

Beware

Ensure that the
application has
permission to write to
the log file location.

7 Click the Start Debugging button, or press F5, to run the
application then enter some text into the top TextBox

8 Click the **WriteBtn** to have your text written into a new
file and see the top TextBox become cleared

9 Click the **ReadBtn** to have the file contents read and see
your text appear in the bottom TextBox

Hot tip

Remove the log file then
click the ReadBtn to
attempt to read from the
missing file – the Catch
statement will appear.

10 Repeat steps 7 and 8 to append more lines of text then
click the **DeleteBtn** to remove the file and text content

Streaming lines of text

The Visual Basic **System.IO** class can be used to import data and files into an application as a "stream". A stream is more flexible than a file as it can be searched and manipulated. A stream is first created as a new **System.IO.FileStream** object that specifies the file to work with and the operation to perform as its parameters. A new **System.IO.StreamReader** object can then be created to read from an opened file in a variety of ways – its **ReadToEnd()** method will read the entire file. It is important to then release the StreamReader and FileStream using their **Dispose()** method.

 1   Add to a Form an OpenFileDialog, a TextBox and two Button controls named **OpenBtn** and **PrintBtn**

2   Double-click on the **OpenBtn** to open the Code Editor then add this code to the Declarations section
Dim txt As String

3   Now add the following code to the **OpenBtn** control's Click event-handler

```
If OpenFileDialog1.ShowDialog = _
        Windows.Forms.DialogResult.OK Then
Dim stream As New System.IO.FileStream _
(OpenFileDialog1.FileName, System.IO.FileMode.Open)
Dim reader As New System.IO.StreamReader(stream)
txt = reader.ReadToEnd()
reader.Dispose() : stream.Dispose()
TextBox1.Text = txt
End If
```

Hot tip

Two statements can appear on a single line if they are separated by a colon character, as here.

4   Run the application then click the **OpenBtn** and browse to select a text file for display in the TextBox

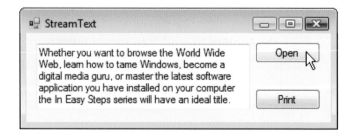

150

Adding Print ability

1 Add both a PrintDialog and PrintDocument component from the Printing section of the Toolbox

2 Double-click on the PrintBtn and add the following code to its Click event-handler

```
PrintDialog1.AllowSomePages = True
PrintDialog1.ShowHelp = True
If PrintDialog1.ShowDialog = _
        Windows.Forms.DialogResult.OK Then
        If txt <> "" Then
        PrintDocument1.Print()
        End If
End If
```

Don't forget

The PrintDialog component lets your application launch the Windows Print dialog – but you need to add a PrintDocument component to actually print anything.

This Sub routine configures the Print dialog then, if the **txt** variable is not empty, calls the **Print()** method of the PrintDocument1 component. This is not enough to print by itself – it merely fires a **PrintPage** event whose event-handler must be coded to make the application print out the text.

3 Double-click on the PrintDocument1 icon in the Form Designer's component tray to open the Code Editor in its PrintPage event-handler and type this code

```
e.Graphics.DrawString(txt, Me.Font, Brushes.Black, _
e.MarginBounds, StringFormat.GenericTypographic)
```

In this code the letter "e" is specified in the event-handler's parameters to represent a **PrintPageEventArgs** object that uses the **Graphics.DrawString()** method to print the text.

4 Click the Start Debugging button, or press F5, to run the application and use the **OpenBtn** to choose a text file then click the **PrintBtn** to send it to your printer

Beware

Further code would need to be added to the PrintPage event-handler to allow the printer to handle multiple pages.

151

Reading Excel spreadsheets

Data contained within an Excel spreadsheet can be imported into an application where the value of each cell can be conveniently stored in a two-dimensional array, representing rows and columns. This allows each individual cell to be addressed using the same row and column number that it has in the spreadsheet – for instance, cell(2,3) could address the third cell on the second row.

1 Create an Excel Workbook called "Data.xlsx", enter values like those below, then save it in your Documents directory

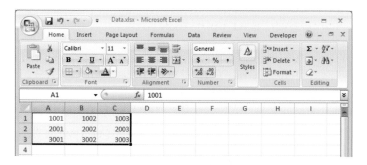

2 Start a new Windows Forms Application and add three ListBox controls, three Labels, and a Button to the Form

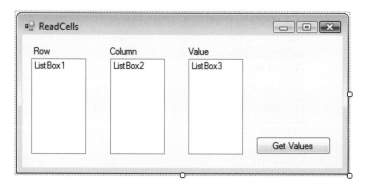

Hot tip

Refer to page 136 for an illustration of the References dialog – compare the similarities in this example with the VBA example listed there.

3 Click Project, Add Reference to launch the Add Reference dialog then choose the Microsoft Excel Object Library item on the COM tab and click OK

4 Press F7 to open the Code Editor then create a path variable to the spreadsheet in the Declarations section
Dim mySS As String = "C:\Users\Mike\Documents\Data.xlsx"

...cont'd

5. Double-click on the Button control to open the Code
Editor and type this code into its Click event-handler

```
Dim row, col, finalRow, finalCol As Integer
Dim xl = CreateObject("Excel.Application")
xl.Workbooks.Open( mySS )
xl.Worksheets("Sheet1").Activate()
finalRow = xl.ActiveSheet.UsedRange.Rows.Count
finalCol = xl.ActiveSheet.UsedRange.Columns.Count
Dim vals(finalRow, finalCol) As String
```

This opens the Worksheet, counts the number of used rows and
columns, then create a two-dimensional array of the same size.

6. Add this loop to assign the cell values to the array
elements and to display them in the ListBoxes

```
For row = 1 To finalRow
        For col = 1 To finalCol
        vals(row, col) = _
                Str(xl.ActiveSheet.Cells(row, col).Value)
        ListBox1.Items.Add(row)
        ListBox2.Items.Add(col)
        ListBox3.Items.Add( vals(row, col) )
        Next col
Next row
```

7. Finally, add these two lines to release the resources then
run the application and click the Button

```
xl.Workbooks.Close()
xl = Nothing
```

Don't forget

Many examples in
this book benefit by
enclosure in a Try Catch
statement but they are
not listed in order to
save space – add one to
this example to catch the
exception that would be
thrown if the Worksheet
could not be read.

Hot tip

See page 63 for more on
multi-dimensional arrays.

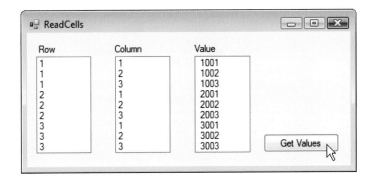

Reading XML files

The Visual Basic **System.Xml** object can be used to easily import data into an application from an XML document. A container for the data is first created as a **System.Xml.XmlDocument** object then the data is loaded into it using its **Load()** method to copy data from the XML document file.

A **System.Xml.XmlNodeList** can then create an **Item()** array of all the elements in the Xml document. Individual elements can be addressed by stating their name as the parameter to the **SelectSingleNode()** method of the **Item()** array, and the value contained within that element retrieved by its **InnerText** property.

Open any plain text editor, such as Notepad, and create an XML document with elements like those below – name it **books.xml** and save it in the Documents folder

Don't forget

You can download the XML document, along with all the other files used in this book, from www.ineasysteps.com.

```
books.xml - Notepad

File  Edit  Format  View  Help

<?xml version="1.0" encoding="utf-8" standalone="yes" ?>

<shelf>

        <book>
                <isbn>978-1-84078-351-3</isbn>
                <title>Linux In Easy Steps</title>
                <author>Mike McGrath</author>
                <class>Operating Systems</class>
        </book>

        <book>
                <isbn>978-1-84078-316-2</isbn>
                <title>Windows Vista In Easy Steps</title>
                <author>Harshad Kotecha</author>
                <class>Operating Systems</class>
        </book>

        <book>
                <isbn>978-1-84078-346-9</isbn>
                <title>Java In Easy Steps</title>
                <author>Mike McGrath</author>
                <class>Programming</class>
        </book>

        <book>
                <isbn>978-1-84078-314-8</isbn>
                <title>Web Design In Easy Steps</title>
                <author>Richard Quick</author>
                <class>Web Development</class>
        </book>

        <book>
                <isbn>978-1-84078-337-7</isbn>
                <title>XML In Easy Steps</title>
                <author>Mike McGrath</author>
                <class>Web Development</class>
        </book>

</shelf>
```

2 Start a new Windows Forms Application and add a listBox and a Button to the Form

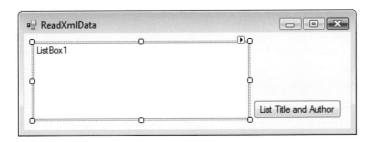

3 Double-click on the Button to open the Code Editor and type this code into its Click event-handler to create an XmlDocument object from the XML file
```
Dim doc As New System.Xml.XmlDocument
doc.Load( "C:\Users\Mike\Documents\books.xml" )
```

4 Add the following code to create an XmlNodeList from the <book> elements and their nested elements
```
Dim nodes As System.Xml.XmlNodeList
nodes = doc.SelectNodes( "shelf/book" )
```

5 Now add a loop to display the text contained in each <title> and <author> element, then run the application
```
Dim counter = 0
Do Until counter = nodes.Count
ListBox1.Items.Add(nodes.Item(counter) _
  .SelectSingleNode("title").InnerText & vbTab _
& nodes.Item(counter) _
  .SelectSingleNode("author").InnerText & vbCrLf)
counter += 1
Loop
```

Hot tip

Notice how the Count property of the XmlNodeList is used to set the limit of the loop.

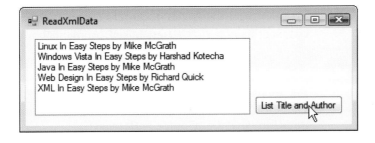

Creating an XML dataset

Visual Basic provides specialized components for working with data in table format, such as that contained in XML elements or database tables. These components can be found in the Toolbox under the "Data" heading.

The DataSet component can be added to an application to create a table in the system memory that can be loaded with data from any suitable source. Most often it is convenient to display the table data in the interface using a DataGridView component. This allows the data stored in memory to be dynamically manipulated within the application then written back to a file.

1   Start a new Windows Forms Application and add a DataGridView component and two Buttons to the Form – name the Buttons **ReadBtn** and **WriteBtn**

Don't forget

The document file books.xml must be located in the Documents directory – adjust the path to suit your system.

2   Double-click on the **DataSet** item in the Toolbox then choose the **Untyped DataSet** option in the Add DataSet dialog and click OK – see the DataSet icon appear on the component tray in the Form Designer

3   Double-click the **ReadBtn** to open the Code Editor then type this code into its Click event-handler to create a DataSet from the XML document shown on page 154
```
DataSet1.ReadXml( "C:\Users\Mike\Documents\books.xml" )
```

4   Add this code to load those elements nested under the <book> element from the DataSet into the DataGridView control
```
DataGridView1.DataSource = DataSet1
DataGridView1.DataMember = "book"
```

5 Return to the Form Designer then double-click the **WriteBtn** and add this code to its Click event-handler
DataSet1.WriteXml("C:\Users\Mike\Documents\books.xml")

6 Click Start Debugging, or press F5, to run the application then click the **ReadBtn** to load the DataSet data into the DataGridView control

	isbn	title	author	class
▶	978-1-84078-351-3	Linux In Easy Steps	Mike McGrath	Operating Systems
	978-1-84078-316-2	Windows Vista In Easy Steps	Harshad Kotecha	Operating Systems
	978-1-84078-346-9	Java In Easy Steps	Mike McGrath	Programming
	978-1-84078-314-8	Web Design In Easy Steps	Richard Quick	Web Development
	978-1-84078-337-7	XML In Easy Steps	Mike McGrath	Web Development
*				

XmlDataSet — Read XML / Write XML

The DataGridView control displays the element name as the heading for each column and the element content on each row of that column. Initially the first cell on the first row is in focus but you can click on any other cell to move the focus. When you double-click the cell in focus it changes into edit mode where you can update its content.

7 Add another row of data to the last row of the table then click the **WriteBtn** control to save the amended data

	isbn	title	author	class
▶	978-1-84078-351-3	Linux In Easy Steps	Mike McGrath	Operating Systems
	978-1-84078-316-2	Windows Vista In Easy Steps	Harshad Kotecha	Operating Systems
	978-1-84078-346-9	Java In Easy Steps	Mike McGrath	Programming
	978-1-84078-314-8	Web Design In Easy Steps	Richard Quick	Web Development
	978-1-84078-337-7	XML In Easy Steps	Mike McGrath	Web Development
▶		Visual Basic In Easy Steps	Mike McGrath	Programming

XmlDataSet — Read XML / Write XML

8 Restart the application then click the **ReadBtn** to once more load the XML data into the DataGridView control – see that the row you added has been preserved

Reading RSS feeds

Live XML data can be imported from outside the local system into a Visual Basic application using a Really Simple Syndication (RSS) feed. This delivers the XML data as a stream that can be stored within a **System.Xml.XmlDocument** object, like that used to store data from an XML file on page 155.

Hot tip

You can find the GroupBox control in the Containers section of the Toolbox.

1. Start a new Windows Application then add a GroupBox Label, Button, and TextBox control to the Form

2. Name the TextBox as "ZipCode" and set its Text property to "10021" – a New York City Zip code. Arrange the controls so your Form looks like this

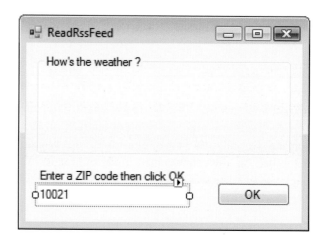

Beware

This example relies upon the format of an external XML document – if the format gets changed it may need amendment to run correctly. You can discover the latest details about the Yahoo RSS weather feed online at http://developer.yahoo. com/weather.

3. To create a request to the Yahoo Weather RSS Feed for the Zip code above double-click on the Button and type the following code into its Click event-handler

```
Dim rssUrl = _
        "http://xml.weather.yahoo.com/forecastrss?p=" _
        + ZipCode.Text
Dim rssRequest As System.Net.WebRequest = _
        System.Net.WebRequest.Create(rssUrl)
```

4. Save the response data into a Stream object by adding these two statements

```
Dim rssResponse As System.Net.WebResponse = _
        rssRequest.GetResponse()
Dim rssStream As System.IO.Stream = _
        rssReponse.GetResponseStream()
```

5 Type the code below to load the saved data stream into an XMLDocument object

```
Dim rssDoc As New System.Xml.XmlDocument
rssDoc.Load(rssStream)
```

6 Create an XmlNodeList under the <channel> element of the XmlDocument object by adding these lines

```
Dim nodes As System.Xml.XmlNodeList
nodes = rssDoc.SelectNodes("/rss/channel")
```

7 Now add this code to display the content contained in the <title> element of the XmlDocument object

```
GroupBox1.Text = _
nodes.Item(0).SelectSingleNode("title").InnerText
```

8 Run the application and click the OK button to test the RSS request – after a short delay see the GroupBox Text property change to the title of the response document

When the application is able to retrieve the title from the XML response document you can proceed to add further code, as described on the next page, to extract information from the document about the current weather conditions.

Hot tip

You need an Internet connection to run this application successfully.

159

Don't forget

Change the value in the TextBox to any other valid US Zip code then click OK to see the title change again – for instance, try 90021.

Addressing XML attributes

The XML response document sent from Yahoo Weather, in response to the RSS request made by the application on the previous page, contains information about the current weather conditions for the specified Zip code.

The details are assigned to attributes of XML elements that each have a **yweather:** namespace prefix. To access XML namespace elements in Visual Basic it is necessary to first create an **XmlNamespaceManager** object then specify the namespace name and URL as parameters to its **AddNamespace()** method. Once an **XmlNamespaceManager** has been created you simply add its name as a second parameter to each **SelectSingleNode()** call.

1. Add three TextBoxes and three Label controls to the Form in the previous example

2. Name the TextBox controls **Climate**, **Temperature**, and **Humidity** then set the Text property of each Label control accordingly

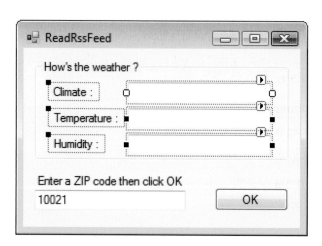

Hot tip

Information, such as the namespace URL, are given in the instructions provided by Yahoo on how to use their RSS Weather feed.

3. Double-click on the OK Button to open the Code Editor and append the following code after the earlier code in its Click event-handler to create an XmlNamespaceManager

```
Dim nsMgr = New _
System.Xml.XmlNameSpaceManager(rssDoc.NameTable)
nsMgr.AddNameSpace("yweather", _
        "http://xml.weather.yahoo.com/ns/rss/1.0")
```

4 Add this code to display the current weather condition

```
Climate.Text = rssDoc.SelectSingleNode( _
"/rss/channel/item/yweather:condition/@text", _
        nsMgr).InnerText
```

5 Add this code to display the current temperature

```
Temperature.Text = rssDoc.SelectSingleNode( _
"/rss/channel/item/yweather:wind/@chill", _
        nsMgr).InnerText + " F"
```

Hot tip

Notice how the @ character is used here in the URL to denote the name of an attribute.

6 Add this code to display the current humidity

```
Humidity.Text = rssDoc.SelectSingleNode( _
"/rss/channel/item/yweather:atmosphere/@humidity", _
        nsMgr).InnerText + " %"
```

7 Surround the entire code inside the Click event-handler with a Try Catch statement – to catch the exception that will be thrown in the event that the RSS feed is not accessible

8 Run the application then click the OK button to retrieve the current weather information for the specified Zip code from the RSS feed

Don't forget

You can see more about Try Catch statements on page 106.

Summary

- The **My.Computer.FileSystem** object can be used to read and write files on your computer

- A **System.IO.Stream** object can store text that has been read from a local file or external source, such as a web response

- It is important to dispose of **System.IO.Stream** and **System.IO.StreamReader** objects after they have been used

- The **Print()** method of a **PrintDocument** component does not actually send data to your printer – it only fires a **PrintPage** event whose event-handler must be coded in order to print

- Data imported from an Excel spreadsheet can best be stored in a two-dimensional array representing rows and columns

- The **System.Xml.XmlDocument** object is used to store a representation of an XML document

- A **System.Xml.XmlNodeList** object creates an **Item()** array of elements selected from a **System.Xml.XmlDocument**

- The **InnerText** property of a node contains the actual content of that element

- A **DataSet** component creates a table in system memory that can be loaded with data from any suitable source

- It is often convenient to display **DataSet** table data in a **DataGridView** component – where it can be modified then written from system memory back to the original source

- An application can request an RSS feed using a **System.Net.WebRequest** object

- A **System.Net.WebResponse** object handles the response received after requesting an RSS feed

- XML elements that have a namespace prefix can be addressed after creating a **System.Xml.NamespaceManager** object

10 Employing databases

This chapter introduces databases and demonstrates how to add powerful database functionality to a Visual Basic application with SQL Server.

An introduction to databases

Databases are simply convenient storage containers that store data in a structured manner. Every database is composed of one or more tables that structure the data into organized rows and columns. This makes it easy to reference and manipulate the data. Each database table column has a label to identify the data stored within the table cells in that column. Each row is an entry called a "record", that places data in each cell along that row like this:

MemberID	Forename	Surname
1	John	Smith
2	Ann	Jones
3	Mike	McGrath

The rows of a database table are not automatically arranged in any particular order so they can be sorted alphabetically, numerically, or by any other criteria. It is important, therefore, to have some means to identify each record in the table. The example above allocates a "MemberID" for this purpose and this unique identifier is known as the **Primary Key** for that table.

Storing data in a single table is useful but relational databases with multiple tables introduce more possibilities by allowing the stored data to be combined in a variety of ways. For example, the table below could be added to the database containing the table shown above.

Beware

Spaces are not allowed in label names – so you should use "MemberID" instead of "Member ID".

VideoID	Title	MemberID
1	Titanic	2
2	Fantasia	3
3	Star Wars	1

The table lists video titles sorted numerically by "VideoID" and describes a relationship linking each member to the video they have rented – John (MemberID 1) has Star Wars (VideoID 3), Ann (MemberID 2) has Titanic (VideoID 1) and Mike (MemberID 3) has Fantasia (VideoID 2). In this table the

VideoID column has the **Primary Key** values identifying records in this table and the **MemberID** column in this table contains **Foreign Key** values that reference records in the first table.

SQL Server

The SQL Server DataBase Management System (DBMS) that is bundled with Visual Basic adheres to the relational model like other Relational DataBase Management System (RDBMS) software, such as Oracle or IBM DB2. This means that it observes "normalization" rules that you need to be aware of when designing a database.

Data normalization

Normalization rules insist that data is organized efficiently, and without duplication or redundancy, in order to reduce the potential for anomolies when performing data operations. They require each table to have a Primary Key column and permissable data types must be defined for all other columns. This determines whether cells in the column may contain text or numbers, within a specified range, and whether cells may be left empty or not.

In considering the design of a database, normalization sensibly requires data to appear only once – so any repeated data should be moved into its own table then referenced where required. For example, where customer name and address details are repeated in two tables they should be moved to their own table which can then be referenced from each of the two original tables. This makes it easier to update the customer details without the possibility of creating an anomaly by updating just one set of data.

Data integrity

Another important aspect of RDBMS software concerns the preservation of data integrity by prohibiting "orphaned" records. This means that records that are referenced in another table cannot be deleted unless the reference is first deleted. Otherwise the reference would become orphaned as it could not find the data in its "parent" table. For example, where a table of customer order details contains a reference to a record in a table of products the RDBMS software will not allow the product record to be deleted as doing so would render the customer order reference useless.

Hot tip

A Foreign Key always references a Primary Key in another table – name them both alike for easy recognition.

Don't forget

SQL Server gets installed along with Visual Basic – see the installation components on page 11.

Designing a database

The process of database design is typically one of refinement to recognize the rules of normalization. Start out with a single table design for all data fields then move those which are repeating into their own table.

Consider the design for a database to store data about an imaginary range of motorcycles comprising "Sport", "Cruiser", and "Touring" models that are selectively available in "Standard", "Deluxe" and "Classic" versions, and where each model/version has a unique price. A single **Bikes** table of the entire range, plus a column for individual notes, might look like this:

BikeID	Model	Version	Price	Note
1	Sport	Standard	4995	
2	Sport	Deluxe	5495	
3	Cruiser	Standard	7995	
4	Cruiser	Deluxe	8495	
5	Cruiser	Classic	8995	
6	Touring	Standard	9495	
7	Touring	Classic	9995	

Don't forget

A Primary Key uniquely identifes a row within a database table – so a Primary Key value should never be changed.

The **BikeID** column provides a unique identifier for each row and can be set as the **Primary Key** for the table. The **Price** column contains unique values and all cells in the **Note** column are initially empty. **Model** and **Version** columns both contain repeating data in contravention of the normalization rules so they should each be moved into separate tables like those below:

ModelID	Model
1	Sport
2	Cruiser
3	Touring

VersionID	Version
1	Standard
2	Deluxe
3	Classic

The **ModelID** and **VersionID** columns provide a unique identifier for each row and can be set as the **Primary Key** (PK) for their table – and they can also be used as a **Foreign Key** (FK) in the refined Bikes table below:

BikeID [PK]	ModelID [FK]	VersionID [FK]	Price	Note
1	1	1	4995	
2	1	2	5495	
3	2	1	7995	
4	2	2	8495	
5	2	3	8995	
6	3	1	9495	
7	3	3	9995	

In considering permissable data types for each column, in line with normalization rules, the **BikeID**, **ModelID**, **VersionID**, and **Price** columns should each allow only integer values. The **Model** and **Version** columns should only allow up to ten characters and the **Note** column should allow up to, say, fifty various characters. All except the **Note** column are required to contain data – in database terms they should be "Not Null". The Database Diagram below illustrates these data constraints and the table relationships:

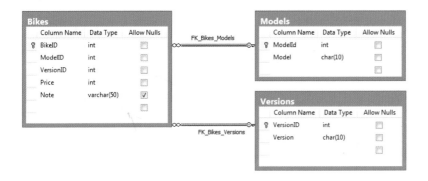

Beware

In setting data constraints consider future eventualities – might a new Model or Version perhaps have a name longer than 10 characters?

This design is used on the ensuing pages to create a SQL Server database and a Visual Basic application that can communicate with it to dynamically retrieve and manipulate data.

Creating a database

SQL Server is well integrated with Visual Basic so you can easily create a new database from within the IDE.

1 Start a new Windows Forms Application in Visual Basic and name it **BikesApplication**

2 Click View, Solution Explorer, or press Ctrl+Alt+L, to open the Solution Explorer window

3 In the Solution Explorer window, right-click on the top project icon then choose Add, New Item from the context menu to launch the Add New Item dialog

4 In the Add New Item dialog select the "Server-based Database" icon, type BikesDatabase.mdf in the name field, then click the Add button

Beware

Be sure to click the Cancel button to close the Data Source Configuration Wizard dialog – not the Finish button.

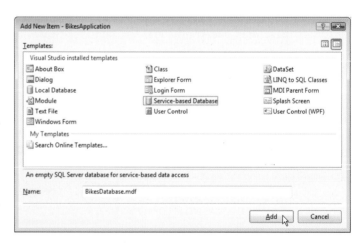

5 When the Data Source Configuration Wizard dialog appears just click its Cancel button for now

Connecting to a database

1 In Solution Explorer, right-click the **BikesDatabase.mdf** icon that has been added, then choose Open from the context menu to open the Database Explorer window

Hot tip

You can also open the Database Explorer window by choosing View, Database Explorer on the Menu Bar, or with a double-click on the BikesDatabase.mdf icon in Solution Explorer.

2 Examine the **BikesDatabase.mdf** icon in Database Explorer and you should see it has an "electric-cord" below it to indicate you are connected to that database

3 Right-click the **BikesDatabase.mdf** icon in Database Explorer then choose Close Connection from the context menu – see the icon change to have a red X below it

4 Right-click the **BikesDatabase.mdf** icon in Database Explorer then choose Refresh to reconnect to the database – see the icon has the "electric-cord" below it once more to indicate you are connected again

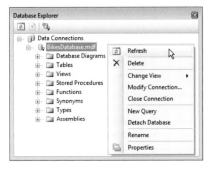

Beware

This chapter builds a complete database application. To recreate this application it is important you carefully follow each step, in the same sequence, in order to avoid errors later.

5 To test the connection choose Modify Connection to launch the Modify Connection dialog then click its Test Connection button – see the Connection Succeeded confirmation dialog appear

6 Click the OK button on both dialogs to close them

169

Adding database tables

Having created the **BikesDatabase** database on the previous page, you can begin to add the **Bikes, Models,** and **Versions** tables from the database design on page 167 by creating the tables and setting the Primary Key column for each table.

1 In Database Explorer right-click on the Tables icon and choose Add New Table from the context menu to open the Table Designer window and tool bar

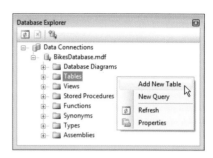

2 In Table Designer, type **BikeID** in the field below the Column Name heading to name the column

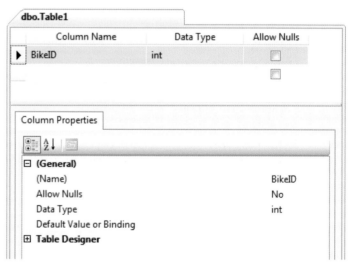

Don't forget

When working with Table Designer you can close the Form Designer window to tidy the IDE.

3 Click below the Data Type heading then choose the **int** item from the dropdown options to allow only integer data in this column

4 Ensure that the Allow Nulls checkbox is not checked so empty cells will not be allowed in this column

5 Click the **Set Primary Key** button on the Table Designer toolbar to make this column the table's Primary Key

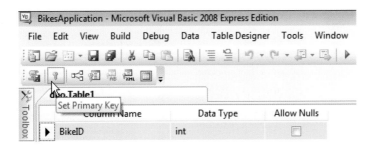

Beware

The Table Designer menu and toolbar are only visible when you have Table Designer open.

6 In the Column Properties window, expand Identity Specification under the Table Designer menu then set the **Is Identity** property to Yes – to have the column automatically number its rows

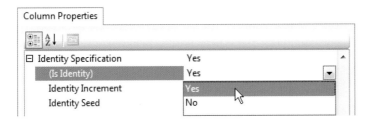

7 Click File, Save Table, or press Ctrl+S, to launch the Choose Name dialog then name this table **Bikes** and click the OK button

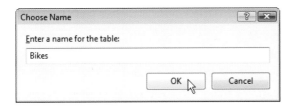

Hot tip

You can double-click any table icon in Database Explorer to reopen that table in Table Designer.

8 Repeat these steps to create the **Models** table with **ModelID** and the **Versions** table with **VersionID** – and see icons appear in Database Explorer for each new table

171

Defining table columns

Having created the **Bikes**, **Models**, and **Versions** tables on the previous page, you can begin to define other columns for each table, setting their Column Name, Data Type and Allow Nulls.

1 In Database Explorer, right-click on the **Bikes** table icon then choose Open Table Definition from the context menu to open it in Table Designer

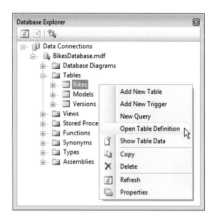

2 Click the next line under the Column Name heading, below the box containing the **BikeID** name, then type **ModelID** to name that column, set the data type to **int** and uncheck the Allow Nulls checkbox

3 Repeat step 2 to define the **VersionID** and **Price** columns

4 Add a column named **Note**, set the data type to **varchar(50)** and do check the Allow Nulls checkbox so the completed table definition looks like this

Don't forget

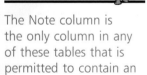

The Note column is the only column in any of these tables that is permitted to contain an empty cell.

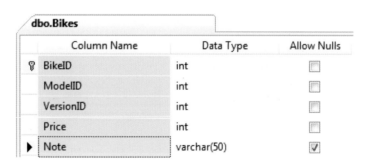

dbo.Bikes

Column Name	Data Type	Allow Nulls
🔑 BikeID	int	☐
ModelID	int	☐
VersionID	int	☐
Price	int	☐
▶ Note	varchar(50)	✓

5 In Database Explorer, double-click on the **Models** table icon to open it in Table Designer

6 Click the next line under the Column Name heading, below the box containing the **ModelID** name, then type **Model** to name that column, set the data type to **char(10)** and uncheck the Allow Nulls checkbox

dbo.Models		
Column Name	Data Type	Allow Nulls
ModelId	int	☐
▶ Model	char(10)	☐

7 In Database Explorer, double-click on the **Versions** table icon, or choose Open Table Definition from the right-click context menu, to open it in Table Designer

8 Click the next line under the Column Name heading, below the box containing the **VersionID** name, then type **Version** to name that column, set the data type to **char(10)** and uncheck the Allow Nulls checkbox

dbo.Versions		
Column Name	Data Type	Allow Nulls
VersionID	int	☐
▶ Version	char(10)	☐

9 Click File, Save All, or press the Save All button, to save the project and all the updated table definitions – expand the tables in Database Explorer to see all the defined columns you have created

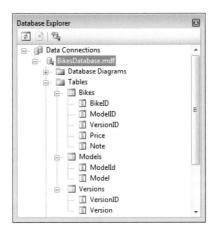

Hot tip

When a table is open in Table Designer you can click View, Properties Window to discover properties of that table.

Making table relationships

Having defined all the table columns on the previous page, you can now establish the relationship between the tables to recognize the links for the **Bikes** table's **ModelId** column to the **Models** table, and its **VersionID** column to the **Versions** table.

1 In Database Explorer, right-click on the Database Diagrams icon then choose Add New Diagram from the context menu

2 When a dialog box appears asking if you want to create required objects click the Yes button – after a short delay the Add Table dialog will appear

3 Select all three tables (**Bikes, Models, Versions**) in the Add Tables list then click the Add button to create a diagram – click Close to close the Add Tables dialog

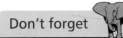
Don't forget

You can automatically rearrange the tables by choosing Arrange Tables on the Database Diagram menu.

4 Click the Save All button, or press Ctrl+Shift+S, to save the diagram and the Choose Name dialog will request a name – type **BikesDiagram** then click OK

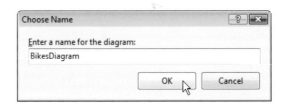

The relationship to be established in this case is to create a Foreign Key for the **ModelId** and **VersionID** columns in the **Bikes** table, linking them to their respective tables.

5 In the Database Diagram click on the yellow key button in the **Models** table then drag the cursor to the **ModelID** column in the **Bikes** table – a line gets drawn between the two points indicating the linked relationship

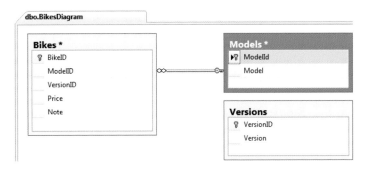

6 Release the mouse button and see two dialogs appear. In the Tables and Columns dialog check that **ModelID** is the common link then click OK in both dialogs to close them

7 Now click the yellow key button in the **Versions** table and drag the cursor to the **VersionID** column in the **Bikes** table – see another line get drawn in the diagram

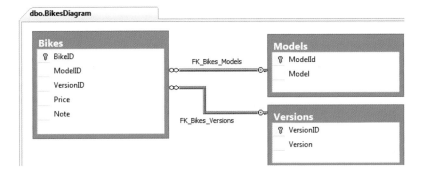

8 Close both dialogs again then click the Save All button, or press Ctrl+Shift+S, to add the relationships to the database and click Yes when asked if you want to save

Entering table data

Having established the tables relationship on the previous page, you can now begin to enter actual data records into each table.

1. In Database Explorer, expand the Tables tree then right-click on the **Models** table icon and choose Show Table Data from the context menu to open the **Models** table in the Table Data window

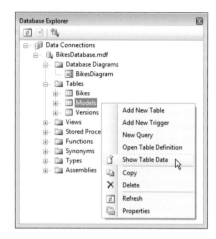

2. Click under the **Model** heading and type **Sport** then press Tab to move to the **Model** column on the next row – see numbering automatically appear in the **ModelID** column as you specified when creating the table

3. Type **Cruiser** on the second row and **Touring** on the third row so the table looks like this – then click the X button to close this window

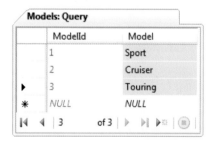

	ModelId	Model
	1	Sport
	2	Cruiser
▶	3	Touring
✳	NULL	NULL

Models: Query

|◀ ◀ | 3   of 3 | ▶ ▶| ▶※ | ▣ |

Hot tip

You can move from row to row using the arrow buttons at the bottom of the Table Data window.

4. Open the **Versions** Table Data window then, under the **Version** column, enter **Standard** on the first row, **Deluxe** on the second and **Classic** on the third row

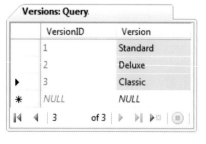

Versions: Query

	VersionID	Version
	1	Standard
	2	Deluxe
▶	3	Classic
✳	NULL	NULL

|◀ ◀ | 3   of 3 | ▶ ▶| ▶※ | ▣ |

5 Open the **Bikes** table in the Table Data window then click under the **ModelID** heading and enter the data from the colored table on page 167 – use the Tab key to move through the cells to enter **ModelId**, **VersionID**, and **Price** data so that the table looks like this

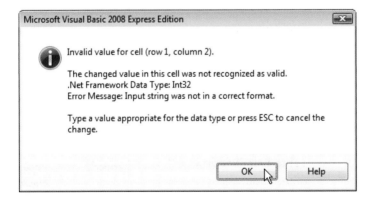

BikeID	ModelID	VersionID	Price	Note
1	1	1	4995	NULL
2	1	2	5495	NULL
3	2	1	7995	NULL
4	2	2	8495	NULL
5	2	3	8995	NULL
6	3	1	9495	NULL
7	3	3	9995	NULL
* NULL	NULL	NULL	NULL	NULL

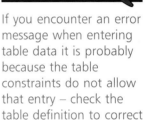

Hot tip

If you encounter an error message when entering table data it is probably because the table constraints do not allow that entry – check the table definition to correct the problem.

6 To test that the table constraints are working correctly click the **ModelID** cell on row 1 and change its value to text then press the Tab key – an error dialog should appear complaining that this entry is invalid

Microsoft Visual Basic 2008 Express Edition

Invalid value for cell (row 1, column 2).

The changed value in this cell was not recognized as valid.
.Net Framework Data Type: Int32
Error Message: Input string was not in a correct format.

Type a value appropriate for the data type or press ESC to cancel the change.

OK   Help

Don't forget

You can test the Foreign Key constraints are working by trying to delete any row from the Models or Versions table – you should see a dialog appear saying you cannot do so.

7 Press the Esc key to revert back to the original cell value then click the X button to close the Table Data window

Creating a database dataset

Having created a database with related tables and data entries, over the last few pages, you can now proceed to develop the **BikesApplication** program to incorporate the data as a dataset.

1 Click Data, Add New Data Source on the Menu Bar to launch the Data Source Configuration Wizard dialog

2 Select the Database icon then click Next to proceed

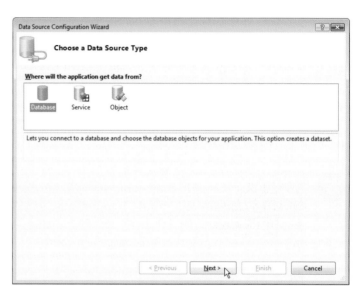

You can click the + button to view the Connection string.

3 Select **BikesDatabase.mdf** as the chosen connection in the dropdown list, then click Next

4 Check the "Yes, save the connection as" checkbox, then click Next again

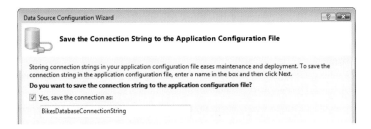

5 Check the Tables checkbox to include all the database tables in the dataset, then click the Finish button

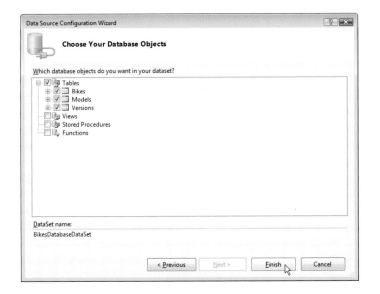

6 In Solution Explorer see that the dataset has been created as a new XML Schema Document and the application configuration is stored in an XML document named **app.config**

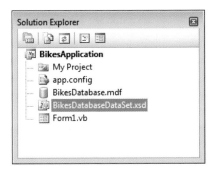

Don't forget

A dataset is an in-memory representation of the tables in the database which can be manipulated before writing data back to the tables.

Adding form data controls

Having created a database data set on the previous page you are now ready to add controls to the Form to display the data.

 Ensure Form Designer is open then click Data, Show Data Sources to open the Data Sources window

Select the **Bikes** icon then click on the dropdown arrow button that appears and choose the Details option

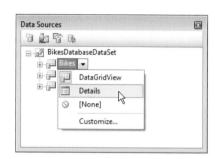

Expand the **Bikes** tree, select any item then click the arrow button that appears to see a list of possible controls. Choose ComboBox for **ModelID** and **VersionID**, and Textbox for the rest

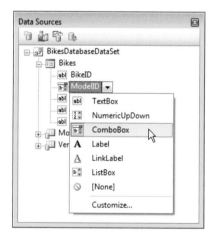

Get ready to experience one of the most stunning features in Visual Basic! Click on the **Bikes** icon in the Data Sources window then drag it across the IDE and drop it onto the Form in Form Designer – see lots of controls get automatically added to the Form and see these five items get added to the Component tray

BikesBindingSource   BikesTableAdapter

TableAdapterManager   BikesBindingNavigator   BikesDatabaseDataSet

...cont'd

Two ComboBox
controls and three
Textbox controls
are added to the
Form, as specified
in the Data Sources
dropdown list,
plus a navigation
ToolStrip and
labels matching the column headings.

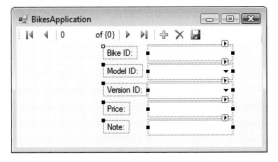

The items added to the Component Tray are non-visual
components to manage the data flow:

● **TableAdapterManager** is the top-level component that
coordinates the update operations of TableAdapters

● **TableAdapter** is the data access object that has Fill and
GetData() methods to actually supply data to the controls

● **DataSet** contains data tables of the in-memory representation
of the database tables

● **BindingSource** is an intermediate manager between the dataset
and Form controls

● **BindingNavigator** supports the navigation ToolStrip to move
through the records, and allows data to be added or deleted

(5) Run the application and try out the navigation controls
– see the data appear from the Bikes table

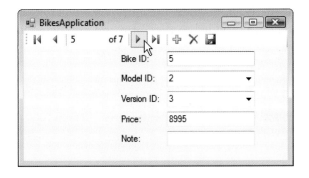

Hot tip

You can view a graphic
representation of the
DataSet – right-click on
the DataSet icon in the
Data Sources window
and choose Edit DataSet
with Designer.

Binding meaningful data

Having added data controls to the Form on the previous page you can now display the data contained in the **Bikes** table but the **ModelID** and **VersionID** fields are still displaying the ID number – not the associated value from the linked table. To correct this so the application displays meaningful data it is necessary to bind the linked tables to those controls.

1 Click on the **Models** table icon in the Data Sources window then drag it to Form Designer and drop it onto the **ModelID** ComboBox control – see **ModelsBindingSource** and **ModelsTableAdapter** items get added to the Component Tray

 ModelsBindingSource   ModelsTableAdapter

2 Click on the **Versions** table icon in the Data Sources window then drag it to Form Designer and drop it onto the **VersionID** ComboBox control – see **VersionsBindingSource** and **VersionsTableAdapter** items get added to the Component Tray

VersionsBindingSource   VersionsTableAdapter

Don't forget

All the data binding settings are made automatically when you bind the linked tables to the ComboBox controls.

3 Click the arrow button on each ComboBox control to reveal their new data binding settings on the Smart Tag

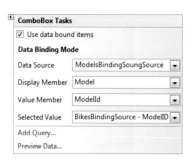

ComboBox Tasks	
☑ Use data bound items	
Data Binding Mode	
Data Source	ModelsBindingSoungSource
Display Member	Model
Value Member	ModelId
Selected Value	BikesBindingSource - ModelID
Add Query...	
Preview Data...	

ComboBox Tasks	
☑ Use data bound items	
Data Binding Mode	
Data Source	VersionsBindingSource
Display Member	Version
Value Member	VersionID
Selected Value	BikesBindingSource - VersionID
Add Query...	
Preview Data...	

The **ModelID** ComboBox control is now bound to **ModelsBindingSource** so will now display the **Model** value, rather than its ID number.

Similarly, the **VersionID** ComboBox is now bound to the **VersionsBindingSource** so will now display the **Version** value, rather than its ID number.

4 Edit the Label control alongside each ComboBox to remove the "ID" text – reflecting the new value these controls will display

5 As the BikeID is not really meaningful to the user set its Visible property to False in the Properties window then delete its Label control

6 Run the application and see meaningful values appear

7 To test the ability to save data permanently back to the database enter some text in the Note field and click the Save Data button – restart the application and see that your text has been preserved

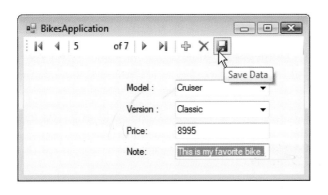

Hot tip

You can also go the projects bin/debug folder and run the executable application there to see that the data is preserved in the database.

Building custom SQL queries

Having added the ability to display meaningful data on the previous page you can now exploit the true power of databases by building custom SQL queries to extract only specific data.

1 Select the **BikesTableAdapter** icon in the Component Tray then choose Add Query from its Smart Tag options to launch the Search Criteria Builder dialog

The Search Criteria Builder dialog displays an SQL query named **FillBy** that is executed by the Form's Load event-handler to populate the navigation ToolStrip and Form fields. This query selects all columns and rows of the **Bikes** table. It can be recreated as a custom SQL query that can be executed to perform the same service whenever the user requires all data to be selected.

2 Change the New Query Name field to "GetAll", then click OK – see another ToolStrip get added to the Form containing a button labelled **GetAll**

3 Select the new ToolStrip then, in the Properties window, set its AutoSize to False and change its MaximumSize and Size properties to resemble a single button 100, 30

To create custom SQL queries that select specific data you can simply edit the default query by appending a qualification clause.

4 Click the **BikesTableAdapter** component icon and choose Add Query to open Search Criteria Builder again

5 Change the New Query Name field to "GetClassics", then append this statement to the Query Text statement **WHERE VersionID = 3**

Select a parameterized query to load data:
- ⦿ New query name: GetClassics
- ○ Existing query name: [▼]

Query Text:
SELECT BikeID, ModelID, VersionID, Price, Note FROM dbo.Bikes WHERE VersionID = 3

6 Click OK to create a ToolStrip for this query and resize it as before to resemble a single button

7 Reopen Search Criteria Builder and create a new Query named "GetCruisers" appending this to the Query Text
WHERE ModelID = 2

8 Resize the new ToolStrip as before, then run the application and click the **GetClassics** button to select data on all **Classic** versions only

BikesApplication
◀◀ ◀ 2 of 2 ▶ ▶▶ ✚ ✕ 💾
GetAll
GetClassics   Model : Touring ▼
GetCruisers   Version : Classic ▼
GetClassics   Price: 9995
Note:

9 Click the **GetAll** button to select all data once more, then click **GetCruisers** to select data on all **Cruiser** models only

BikesApplication
◀◀ ◀ 1 of 3 ▶ ▶▶ ✚ ✕ 💾
GetAll
GetClassics   Model : Cruiser ▼
GetCruisers   Version : Standard ▼
GetCruisers   Price: 7995
Note:

Hot tip

The navigation ToolStrip shows the number of records selected by that query – in this case two Classic versions and three Cruiser models.

Summary

- Databases store data in structured rows and columns making it easy to reference and manipulate data

- Each row in a database table is called a record and must have a **Primary Key** to uniquely identify that record

- A table in a relational databases can address its own records by **Primary Key** and address other tables by **Foreign Key**

- Normalization rules insist that data must not be duplicated within a database and column data types must be defined

- Data integrity is preserved by database constraints

- SQL Server is integrated with Visual Basic to allow databases to be created from within the IDE

- Table constraints are established in the Table Definition

- Setting the **Primary Key** column's **Is Identity** property to Yes will automatically number each row

- Table relationships can be established graphically in a **Database Diagram**

- Table constraints are tested in realtime as Table Data is input

- A database data set is an in-memory representation of the data contained within the database tables

- Drag'n'drop a table from the **Data Sources** window onto a Form to automatically create data controls

- A **BindingSource** manages the data flow between a data set and Form controls

- Drag'n'drop a table from the **Data Sources** window onto a control to bind meaningful data from the table to that control

- A **TableAdapter** has methods to supply data to Form controls and can add custom SQL queries to exploit the true power of databases by selecting specific data

G

J

189

H

K

I

L

Adding a Splash Screen

1 Click Project, Add New Item on the Menu Bar, to launch the Add New Item dialog, then select the Splash Screen icon and click the Add button – see a new Form called **SplashScreen1.vb** get added in Solution Explorer

2 In Solution Explorer right-click on the top project icon then select Properties from the context menu, or click Project, Properties on the Menu Bar, to open the Project Designer window

3 Open the Splash Screen dropdown list at the bottom of the Project Designer window and select **SplashScreen1**

Splash screen:

(None) ▼
(None)
AboutBox1
SplashScreen1

4 Click Start Debugging, or press F5, to run the application and see a splash screen display for about two seconds before the main Form appears

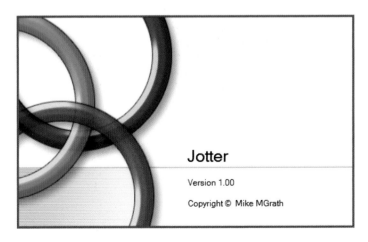

Jotter

Version 1.00

Copyright © Mike MGrath

Don't forget

The Splash Screen and About dialog are similar – both display information from the Assembly Information but less detail is shown in the Splash Screen because it is only displayed briefly.

Controlling multiple forms

Applications sometimes need more than one Form to accommodate the user interface. When the user moves to the second Form the first one can be hidden so any information it contains will remain in memory and reappear when the user returns to that Form. Similarly, the second Form can be hidden so any user input it contains is available to the program when the user returns to the first Form. Alternatively the second Form can be closed when the user returns to the first Form but any user input will then be lost unless it has been stored in variables.

1. Add two Buttons and Labels to a Form so it looks like this and name the yellow Label **ValueLbl**

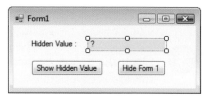

2. Click Project, Add New Item and add another Windows Form to the project

3. Add two Buttons and a TextBox to this Form, naming the Buttons as **HideBtn** and **CloseBtn**

4. In Form Designer double-click on the "Hide Form 1" Button in Form 1 and add this code to its Click event-handler
   Me.Hide()
   Form2.Show()

5. Now double-click on the "Show Hidden Value" Button in Form 1 and add this code to that Click event-handler
   ValueLbl.Text = Form2.TextBox1.Text